FEELING OBLIGATED

Teaching in Neoliberal Times

Feeling Obligated combines theoretical insights with the first-hand experiences of Canadian teachers to illustrate the impact of neoliberalism – the installation of market norms into educational and social policies – on teachers' professional integrity.

Anne M. Phelan and Melanie D. Janzen illustrate the miserable conditions in which teachers teach, their efforts to navigate and withstand those circumstances, and their struggle to respond ethically to students, especially those already marginalized economically and socially. Exploring how educational policies attempt to recast teachers as skilled clinicians, the book revitalizes a conversation about teaching as a vocation wherein the challenge of obligation is of central concern. Haunted by what has already happened and threatened by what may yet occur, *Feeling Obligated* foregrounds the challenge of ethical obligation in teaching and makes a strong case for the revitalization of teaching as a vocation, involving commitment, resolve, and trust in a future yet to come.

ANNE M. PHELAN is a professor in the Department of Curriculum and Pedagogy at the University of British Columbia and an honorary professor at the Education University of Hong Kong.

MELANIE D. JANZEN is a professor in the Department of Curriculum, Teaching, and Learning at the University of Manitoba.

Feeling Obligated

Teaching in Neoliberal Times

ANNE M. PHELAN AND
MELANIE D. JANZEN

UNIVERSITY OF TORONTO PRESS
Toronto Buffalo London

Toronto Buffalo London
utorontopress.com
Printed and bound by CPI Group (UK) Ltd, Croydon, CR0 4YY

ISBN 978-1-4875-5085-1 (cloth)
ISBN 978-1-4875-5086-8 (paper)
ISBN 978-1-4875-5089-9 (EPUB)
ISBN 978-1-4875-5090-5 (PDF)

Library and Archives Canada Cataloguing in Publication

Title: Feeling obligated : teaching in neoliberal times / Anne M. Phelan and Melanie D. Janzen.
Names: Phelan, Anne M., author. | Janzen, Melanie D., author.
Description: Includes bibliographical references and index.
Identifiers: Canadiana (print) 2023047893X | Canadiana (ebook) 20230478964 | ISBN 9781487550851 (cloth) | ISBN 9781487550868 (paper) | ISBN 9781487550899 (EPUB) | ISBN 9781487550905 (PDF)
Subjects: LCSH: Teachers – Professional ethics – Canada. | LCSH: Teaching – Social aspects – Canada. | LCSH: Teaching – Vocational guidance – Canada. | LCSH: Neoliberalism – Canada.
Classification: LCC LB1779.P44 2023 | DDC 174/.937 – dc23

Cover design: Liz Harasymczuk
Cover image: Gino's Premium Images/Alamy Stock Photo

We wish to acknowledge the land on which the University of Toronto Press operates. This land is the traditional territory of the Wendat, the Anishnaabeg, the Haudenosaunee, the Métis, and the Mississaugas of the Credit First Nation.

This book has been published with the help of a grant from the Federation for the Humanities and Social Sciences, through the Awards to Scholarly Publications Program, using funds provided by the Social Sciences and Humanities Research Council of Canada.

University of Toronto Press acknowledges the financial support of the Government of Canada, the Canada Council for the Arts, and the Ontario Arts Council, an agency of the Government of Ontario, for its publishing activities.

Canada Council for the Arts　Conseil des Arts du Canada

Funded by the Government of Canada　Financé par le gouvernement du Canada

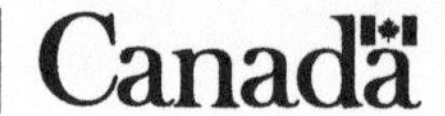

Contents

Acknowledgments vii

Introduction: The "Miserable Conditions" of Teaching 3

1 Precarious Others: Valuing Singularity 27

2 Alienation and Exclusion: Appreciating Proximity 45

3 Shamed and Shaming: Honouring Students 59

4 Destitute and Dying: Preserving Dignity 73

5 Fears and Frustrations: Acknowledging Desire 91

6 Revitalizing Teaching as Vocation 103

Index 125

Acknowledgments

We offer our sincere thanks and dedicate this volume to those teachers who generously gave of their time to talk with us about their experiences of obligation in today's classrooms. The study in which they participated was supported by the Social Sciences and Humanities Research Council of Canada.

Our thanks also to the University of Ottawa Press and Taylor & Francis for permission to reprint the following:

Chapter 1: Precarious Others: Valuing Singularity was previously published by Janzen, M.D. in A.M. Phelan, W.F. Pinar, N. Ng-A-Fook, & R. Kane (Eds.) (2020). *Reconceptualizing Teacher Education: A Canadian Contribution to a Global Challenge*. University of Ottawa Press.

Chapter 2: Alienation and Exclusion: Appreciating Proximity was adapted from a previously published article by Janzen, M., & Phelan, A.M. (2018). Tugging at Our Sleeves: Understanding Experiences of Obligation in Teaching. *Teaching Education, 30*(1), 16–30.

FEELING OBLIGATED

Teaching in Neoliberal Times

Introduction: The "Miserable Conditions" of Teaching

Feeling Obligated: Teaching in Neoliberal Times illustrates and interrogates the experience of teaching in today's Canadian schools.

Working within a global context characterized by political anxieties about declining economic productivity, teachers are at once dedicated to the educational value of teaching (i.e., cultivating students' capacity to lead good and worthwhile lives, in the company of others, in a particular society) *and* compelled "to navigate and withstand often miserable conditions for pursuing it" (Brown, 2017, p. 56). Emphasis on academic achievement, symbolized by test scores, as the sole determinant of teachers' success distorts the educational aims of professional practice, damaging professional integrity, and leaving teachers with a deep feeling of unmet obligation (Clarke & Phelan, 2017). Sidelining teachers' ethical responsibility, the goal of education reform worldwide has been to elevate the importance of capital – human, financial, and corporate – as the value governing all entities big and small, public and private. While education always involves negotiation of diverse values and interests, in such toxic times, in which the moral person has to be destroyed (Benhabib, 2003), the challenge has intensified and the stakes are high; the replacement of democracy with "plutocracy, technocracy, and autocracy" (Brown, 2017, p. 60) is at issue. What does it mean to teach and be a teacher in such times?

Combining theoretical insights with empirical evidence – the first-hand experiences of Canadian teachers – the central argument of this book is that neoliberal *educational* policies attempt to recast teachers as skilled clinicians – stripped of an ethical form of life – by installing market norms in public institutions (Hood, 1991). The problem is magnified by neoliberal *social* policies that seek to maintain the economic status quo rather than promote equity and social responsibility. As such, teachers' ethical response to students, specifically those marginalized economically and socially, is more necessary and more significant than ever. We illustrate the conditions in which teachers teach, the manner of their ethical response to current conditions, and the ensuing struggle to meet their obligation to students while holding on to a modicum of professional integrity. Haunted by what has already happened and threatened by what may yet occur, the book foregrounds the challenge of ethical obligation in teaching and makes a strong case for the revitalization of teaching as a vocation in an era in which the ethical is sidelined in the interest of juridical or legal responsibility.

Our reasons for writing are three-fold: to illustrate the neoliberal material and discursive conditions of teaching as identified by teachers themselves; to theorize teachers' experiences of feeling obligated to students; and, finally, to revitalize a conversation about teaching as a vocation wherein the challenge of obligation is of central concern.

What Teaching Does to Teachers

Neoliberal capitalism in Canada has promoted provincial disinvestment from social and educational programs. As our portrayal of social and educational policy in British Columbia and Manitoba later in this chapter will illustrate, one of the most concerning effects of neoliberalism is the "intensified inequality" (Brown, 2015a, p. 28) in which those who have less are not provided with the resources and supports to counter the effects of their social, historic, and systemic disadvantage. The lack of investment in resources required for students' educational well-being results in transferring the burden of responsibility for both productive outputs (i.e., achievement and credentials as essential to waged work) *and* socially reproductive outputs (i.e., duty of care; sustaining social bonds and shared understandings) from provincial ministries of education to the shoulders of teachers.

Set against this policy backdrop, the stories shared in this volume were gathered from elementary, middle, and secondary public school teachers in Manitoba and British Columbia during the years 2015–18 as part of a research study funded by the Social Sciences and Humanities Research Council of Canada (SSHRC). Our central concern was a familiar one: *what does teaching do to teachers within this historical moment?* The three-year study, titled "The Emotional Toll of Obligation: Teachers' Disengagement from the Profession," was grounded in concerns about teacher attrition. Teacher attrition is often interpreted as a sign of weakness either in the teacher who cannot cope and/or in teacher education programs that fail to sufficiently prepare teachers for their role in equitably educating vulnerable students (Organisation of

Economic Co-operation and Development, 2019; Cochran-Smith et al, 2016; Moore & Slee, 2020). Such studies tend to ignore how diminishing educational provision, wrought by neoliberal policies, means reduced capacity on the part of teachers. By attributing teacher disengagement from the profession, manifesting in burnout, stress leave, sick days, and ultimately greater attrition (Crocco & Costigan, 2007; Schaefer, Long & Clandinin, 2012), the discourse of attrition emphasizes the individual teacher rather than the wider systemic issues – inadequate educational and social welfare funding, for example – at play. Social inequities are not the fault of teachers nor should teachers be held solely responsible for addressing them (Mayer, Goodwin & Mockler, 2021). It is, however, "teachers who interact daily with the most vulnerable in society, children and young people, all the time and especially during this time" (p. 216; emphasis in original).

We conducted in-depth phenomenological interviews with twenty-four teachers who had either left or who had considered leaving teaching. We wanted to elicit teachers' understandings and experiences of obligation in order to trace the various events that generated disengagement from the profession. Participants were invited to respond to a series of prompts that were provided to them in advance of the interview (similar to the methods used in Pitt & Britzman, 2003). The prompts asked participants to describe, for example, a time when they felt frustrated by the expectations of others, had disappointed others, or had felt insufficiently prepared to support children. The interviews sought to solicit participants' reflections on personal, social, and historical narratives related to their decisions to stay or leave, as well as their everyday sense of disengagement from the profession. We also engaged several focus group discussions with school leaders with whom we shared fictionalized narratives based on the teacher interviews. These narratives were fictionalized in the sense the teachers' authorship was minimal. MacIntyre (1984) explains: "The difference between imaginary characters and real ones is not in the narrative form of what they do" but "in the degree of their authorship of that form and of their own deeds" (p. 215 in Conle, 1999, p. 19). Discussion of the fictionalized narratives restored the possibility of teachers' authorship because each reader (focus group member) produced different readings undermining the assumption that we can know in any definitive way what the characters (based on interviewees) mean and what motivates them as they speak and act.

Our focus was consistently on the particulars of teachers' lives and experiences. We conducted hermeneutic readings of both interview and focus group transcripts, drawing the transcripts into a "dialogic encounter" (Schwandt, 2003, p. 292) with one another as well as with other texts such as theories, philosophy, media accounts, and fiction. We read the transcripts individually attending to teachers' accounts of critical episodes; articulation of interior monologues, provision of descriptive vignettes; portrayal of images; retelling of small stories with their own beginning, middle, and end; placement of emphasis; and word choice.

We read and reread the transcripts as a precursor to our shared reflection, discussion, and collaborative re-interpretation. During our discussions we identified larger themes as well as those stories that had a resonance for us both. We recognized that the initial telling of the experience constituted a "truth" (Badiou, 2014) for the teacher telling the story – a truth that not only contained the history of the self who had the experience but also the history of what was experienced as ethical obligation. Our challenge has been to identify and theorize these historical aspects of obligation of which the teacher may not have been conscious earlier (Conle, 1999).

When deciding how to represent our insights we were drawn to narrative fragments that were morally charged (Hansen, 2021), discursively expressive (of thought and feeling), provocative, or poetic (Polkinghorn, 1988; Rogan & de Kock, 2005) and that were helpful in conveying the larger theme of the overall interview. In theorizing narrative fragments, we re-storied them (Phelan & Rüsselbaek Hansen, 2018). Re-storying expands each story into "another spiral of telling, this time by incorporating theory as it is transformed by experience. Theory then becomes lived theory" (Conle, 1999). Theories are "stories that deploy implicit and explicit assumptions, logics, and arguments to weave an account of some aspect of life as it unfolds," writes Schiff (2014, p. 3). Each re-storying/theorizing bears witness to "life's contingencies" (p. 189) and invites consideration of our implication in one another's stories and, consequently, our responsibilities.

Re-storying is not unproblematic, however, because stories, especially those represented by transcript fragments, can become "decontextualized" and "hardened," set loose from their experiential moorings so as to serve agendas "outside their inherent telos which is to express, communicate and understand their own contents" (Conle, 1999, p. 17). In our urgency to illustrate the detrimental effects of many current educational and social policies on teachers and students, we have chosen to identify particular stories. We do not claim that these stories represent the lives of *all* teachers in Canada today; neither do we wish to sensationalize by recounting the most tragic and challenging of events and circumstances. What we wish to assert, however, is that despite "a basic faith in public institutions to serve the public good" (Carson, 2017, p. 37) and a history of strong public support for government-funded schooling in Canada (at least until the end of the twentieth century), we are now finding inequalities and situations that lead dedicated teachers to consider the heart-wrenching decision to leave the profession. Teachers told us stories of daily confrontations with the vulnerability visited upon students via reckless educational and social policies, unwarranted parental idealism, and corporate exploitation of the powerless (Brown, 2017). Teachers' stories bore witness to the ways in which education has become "an intensifier of inequality as it becomes a matter of private investment" (p. 65), rather than a public good. Their stories pave the way for responsive action by policymakers and the wider public.

Witnessing Teachers Bearing Witness

There are two senses in which witnessing is important to this study: *witnessing* as a form of educational inquiry in which we as researchers engaged; and *bearing witness* as a practice of living as a teacher in these times.

Witnessing relates to our desire as researchers to understand teachers' experiences in this historical moment and to interrogate the political and material circumstances in which they carry out their daily work. As such, we gathered eyewitness accounts – testimonials – based on teachers' first-hand knowledge of teaching. The idea of witnessing teachers' experiences and understandings is premised on a genuine belief in teachers and in the importance of teaching; as such, it invites us to orient ourselves to teachers' concerns and to consider up close what those concerns illustrate about teaching and the profession at this historical moment.

As a form of educational inquiry, witnessing is an ethical endeavour, as it calls for "a moral awakening" (Hansen, 2017, p. 7). It asks that we respond to the troubling stories of our times (Pacini-Ketchabaw, 2021). Teachers drew our attention to the erosion of values within educational systems and how this plays out in their daily lives in schools. Neoliberal logics of economization, commodification, and futurization – education as a private good and students as both products and producers – have become regimes of truth in systemic education. The ideals of educational self-formation and social commitment have been sidelined. We are concerned with current conditions and their effects on teachers who are compelled to both comply (as a function of their employment) and resist (as a function of the vocation or calling of the profession) the system in which they work. In this way, witnessing can be a vindication, not in a truth-and justice-seeking way, but rather "to bring truths of human life out of the shadows, to uncover them, to prepare oneself for their disclosure, and to render them for others to see and remember" (Hansen & Sullivan, 2022, p. 157).

While our analysis of teachers' testimonies is shaped by "critical sympathy" (Hansen, 2017, p. 18), our intent is not to suggest "woundedness" as the basis for teacher identity (Brown, 1995). Portraying teachers as helpless, burnt out, or vulnerable to the vicissitudes of more powerful others is, in our view, to further victimize them as being in need of pity and protection by the neoliberal state. Positioning teachers as victims obscures the strength and force of teachers' ethical commitment to students and families.

The power of teachers' ethical obligation takes us to a second conception of witnessing at play in this work – *bearing witness*. Bearing witness is "an orientation toward truth" (Hansen & Sullivan, 2022, p. 157); it yields knowledge that is "a deeper, more felt knowledge and insight into truths of what it is to be human, in all its shades and all its contexts of the beautiful and the appalling" (p. 164).

Teachers bear witness to the personhood of students – the ways in which they experience shame and alienation, for example. Teachers' testimonies bear witness to how the role of teacher is inextricable from the teacher's own personhood; bearing witness to the plight of their students – to what is a unique and particular moment of that life – "brings with it responsibility, response-ability, and ethical responsibility" (Oliver, 2001, p. 91). It is an immensely challenging task to bear witness "to something beyond recognition that can't be seen ... the heart of subjectivity" (p. 483) in their students. It involves refusing to simply "recognize" students in the terms offered by dominant policy discourse, where students' subjectivity is "conferred by those in power on those they deem powerless and disempowered" (Oliver, 2001, p. 24). It is here in the space of the "unknown" and the "unrecognizable" where teachers' ethical obligations to the other become possible. "The 'unrecognizable' is the awakening" (Oliver, 2015, p. 486): "The demands of the ethical are impossible and unconditional and yet they necessarily guide our actions.... [O]ur decisions about what is right and what we ought to do keep us awake at night because there is no easy answer; there is no handy principle to which to appeal. Rather, we must respond to each individual and each situation anew according to its singularity.... Witnessing to what is beyond recognition is central to this impossible justice" (p. 489). Appreciating our obligation to the particularity of each student posits ethics as singular and sets teachers' responses in a necessary tension with politics (policies) as universal. This is evident in the hesitation and urgency to act that characterizes teachers' stories as they navigate between what is expected of them officially – professionally, legally, institutionally – and what they believe is their ethical obligation in particular situations. In bearing witness to unthinkable harms, incomprehensible injustices, and intergenerational trauma, fuelled by corrosive public policy, teachers unsettle the certitudes offered by professional codes of ethics and illustrate that obligation often requires one to be "against ethics" (Caputo, 1993).

"Against Ethics": Theorizing Obligation

We found in John Caputo's writing (2012; 1993) conceptual resources that helped us to identify, understand, and explore teachers' experiences of obligation. In turn, the teachers' stories enlivened Caputo's more abstract musings. Caputo (2012) writes that the ghost that haunts teaching is an "insistent spirit" that "insists" in the midst of what exists – the machinery of schooling – where it provokes teachers' attention. At the same time, the ghost "is all but overwhelmed, nearly invisible, nearly nothing at all" (Caputo, 2012, p. 24). What, on the one hand, could be so strong as to compel teachers and yet so weak as to be almost invisible? What could be so unexpected – often coming out of nowhere and anonymous – and yet feel so close to home, so personal? What could provoke disequilibrium and yet enable balance? What could make such little sense and yet, for some, invoke a feeling of purpose and possibility? Caputo (2012) responds: "Whoever enters the spectral space of the school is answering a call, responding to some spirit calling us together here in common cause. What calls? What does it call for? Who is being called upon? To what future does it call us forth?" (p. 30). The "common cause" is education. The spirit, that which lends teaching its moral integrity, is ethical obligation – the binding responsibility of teachers to respond to the needs and suffering of students. We ask after the character of ethical obligation in teaching, what it looks like in practice, and the emotional toll it takes on those who teach. Paradoxically, while teachers' ethical responsiveness has been sidelined, political circumstances and the resultant miserable conditions in which teachers have to do their work have underscored, more than ever perhaps, the importance of obligation in teaching.

Ethical obligation fixes the teacher to a sense of responsibility and necessitates judgment. These moments require an immediate and often visceral response, void of anticipation and enacted without forethought, to a child who is "angry or mad or crying" and who must be attended to "right now"; a child who has failed the year-end tests and is afraid to encounter his parents; a youth who needs a ride to a homeless shelter; or a group of children who have just witnessed the death of a peer on the playground. It is not the uncertainty of taking action that is at issue (action must be taken), but rather that uncertainty resides in the question of which action to take and to what that action might lead. It is a sense of risk at disrupting what has been deemed acceptable behaviour by the profession or the society at large that evokes anxiety. The anxiety of obligation is a result of recognizing one's responsibility, the fear of failing to meet one's responsibility, the concern of responding inappropriately, and the distress of potential reprimand. It is the uncertainty that resides in obligation that induces an emotional toll on the teacher, dramatically illustrating teaching's occupational risk and reality (Britzman, 2006) but also its vitality.

Currently, obligation in the teaching profession is legislated by codes of professional ethics or statements of professional standards; obligation is seen to rely on professional knowledge and ethical know-how, both of which are deemed recognizable and even, on occasion, verifiable. Such codes and statements are founded upon a rational conception of ethics and of course have a place in professional life. These codes offer "principles that force people to be good;" they clarify concepts, secure judgments, and provide "firm guardrails along the slippery slopes of factical life" (Caputo, 1993, p. 4). The authoritative claim of such codes can, of course, be accepted or rejected as the teacher judges appropriately. However, obligation as *visceral responsiveness* is different from ethics and "is both the 'undoing' of ethics and the possibility of a deconstruction of ethics" (Scott, 1995, p. 250). Teachers are often caught in a space where the universals of ethical codes of conduct – duty to report child neglect or abuse – fail to attend to the particulars of the situation at hand. There is no reasoned interplay between generals (codes of conduct) and particulars (the complexities of the lives of children); the particular takes priority – the teacher's obligation to respond in the moment overturns everything else.

Wotherspoon's (2020) study of the intersection of school and child welfare in this time of Reconciliation in Canada provides a compelling example of the problem of strong ethics. He reports that despite official commitments to acknowledge and address colonial legacies of residential schooling, teachers' professional obligations to fulfil state child welfare and educational objectives continue to position schools as "really dangerous places" (p. 34) for many Indigenous families:

> Findings reveal how intersections across two systems formally devoted to the best interests of children can sometimes produce outcomes that

> undermine foundations for both individual and institutional success. Participants recognized the efforts going into acknowledging and preserving Indigenous languages, knowledge, ceremonies, and traditional parenting practices in some schools. However, misunderstandings and failure among teachers to recognize these and other important forms of cultural capital can prompt some children and parents to silence their voices or suppress aspects of Indigenous and personal identity. Long after the last residential school has closed, schooling remains for many Indigenous children and families a place where exposure to ongoing dangers of family disruption has not disappeared.
>
> (p. 48)

As a "weak" form of ethics, obligation, as we engage it in this study, does not tarry with the law of "duty" but exists "without owing, without ought, without why" (Caputo, 2012, p. 25). As a calling obligation insists in what exists; it "insinuates itself into and unsettles what seems settled" (Caputo, 2012, p. 29) and invites teachers to surrender their autonomy so they can be responsive to others when the unanticipated moment demands. This is because the call comes from the world. However, as Pinar (2019) recognizes, the world also exists inside us – in the voice of conscience that enables each one of us to respond to the other. A calling signals a greater possibility for the teacher and draws her back from mere habitual engagement with students and the world of school. So, while the calling comes from elsewhere and is not within the teacher's own power of choice, she is responsible at some level for the decision to hear the call (Sikka as cited in Pinar, 2019, p. 202). As an ethos or a call, therefore, obligation always haunts teaching and teachers, but perhaps never more than during these times.

Neoliberal Educational and Social Policies in Canada

The miserable material and discursive conditions of teaching in Canada at the time of our study (2015–18) stemmed from a protracted and subtle shift to neoliberalism as a governing rationality across the country since the 1980s. While we focus our discussion on the provinces of British Columbia and Manitoba, it is reflective of the situation in other provinces and territories (see Parker, 2017).

The fundamental tenets of neoliberal economic thought include "private ownership of property, production of goods and services for profit, creation of competitive markets and the division of labour" (Laitsch, 2013, p. 17). Politically, the only legitimate role of the neoliberal state is to protect individual liberty, understood in commercial terms. As such, neoliberalism does "profound damage to democratic practices, cultures, institutions, and imaginaries" (Brown, 2015b). Democratic values are switched from a political to an economic register. Liberty no longer refers to political participation or existential freedom but is reduced to market freedom. Equality means, simply, the right to compete in a world of winners and losers.

Beginning with the "erosion rather than outright dismantling" of the former Keynesian welfare state (McBride & McNutt, 2007, p. 186) under the Mulroney government (1984–93) and proceeding through to the early 2000s, new Canadian policies promoted "economic growth and efficiency through competition, tax reductions, deregulation, trade liberalisation, incentives to the private sector and reductions in the role of government in public expenditures" (Carpenter, Weber & Schugurensky, 2012, p. 147). The upshot was a significant reduction of Canada's social wage and a reduced commitment to social programs.

The shifting ideological environment at the federal level created the conditions by which even social democratic governments at the provincial level drifted in a neoliberal direction (McBride & McNutt, 2007). By the early 2000s, neoliberalism was at full throttle in British Columbia. In 2001, a newly elected liberal government, aligning itself with global, continental, and national influences, began implementing "social and labour policy reforms designed to bring about flexibility, or insecurity, for the workforce and social programme beneficiaries" (McBride & McNutt, 2007, p. 195). Similar impacts were felt in Manitoba, a province generally characterized as politically centrist (Frankel, 2012). Yet, neoliberal-informed legislation and policy – tax incentives for resource extraction investors, privatization of Crown corporations, cuts to personal and corporate taxes, reductions in public-sector jobs, and wage restrictions (Camfield, 2018; Jeannotte, 2010) – have been consistently advanced through a decade of Conservative rule (1988–99) and the subsequent New Democratic Party (NDP) government (1999–2016).

Since 2000, the impact of neoliberal social and educational policies on children and youth in both British Columbia and Manitoba has become increasingly evident in the interrelated areas of *child poverty, children in care, dispossession of women,* and *education funding*. As a result, unequal social realities persist and are evident daily in the public school classroom.

Child Poverty

It is well-known that child poverty negatively effects school outcomes, as well as mental and physical health, both in the short term and over time (de Boer, Rothwell & Lee, 2013). In 2000, a coalition of eighty-five groups concerned with child poverty released a report stating that 18.5 per cent of children in Canada live in poverty and that the social safety net is becoming increasingly weak (Stack, 2006).

From 2000 to 2018, the child poverty rate in British Columbia remained higher than the national average – having risen from 21.9 per cent in 1989 to 27.6 per cent in 2000. While there is evidence of a decrease to 18.5 per cent in 2018, one in five children (0–17 years old) were still living in poverty in BC at that time. Poverty in BC is more prevalent among visible minority groups: new immigrant children experience a 44.9 per cent poverty rate; Arab, Korean, and West Asian children have more than double the risk of poverty compared to non-minority children; and the poverty rate for forty-two First Nations reserves in 2018 was an astounding 40 per cent and even higher in rural reserves at 51.2 per cent. Not surprisingly, there is a correlation between socio-economic characteristics such as income and wealth and early development (First Call BC Child and Youth Advocacy Coalition, 2020).

Poverty rates in Manitoba during the 2000s are similarly dismal, with child poverty rates often the highest in the nation (Social Planning Council of Winnipeg, 2020). The NDP provincial government introduced a poverty reduction strategy in 2009, which it renewed in 2012, titled *All Aboard Poverty Reduction Strategy*, metaphorically inviting the poor to get on board the train to prosperity. The strategy – reflective of neoliberal values and knowledge claims (Frankel, 2012) – did not come with any financial allocation and deflected poverty as a problem of social exclusion, which conveniently detracted from the government's responsibility to provide social welfare programs and instead responsibilized the problem as one of individual lack of education and employability.

Children in Care

Although of concern across Canada, issues related to children in care are particularly distressing in Manitoba, due to the extremely high rates and a grossly disproportionate number being Indigenous (First Nations, Métis, or Inuit). In a province with the largest population of Indigenous peoples in the country, the situation reflects both past practices of the government's paternalistic relationship with Indigenous peoples, which manifested in residential schools and the Sixties Scoop, as well as current-day colonial frameworks evident through the child welfare system (Blackstock, 2007).

In 2003, the Manitoba government passed legislation that was intended to restructure child welfare in order to reflect a collaborative planning and implementation model as recommended by the Aboriginal Justice Inquiry (General Child and Family Services Authority), which became known as "devolution." The move to devolution was positioned as "collaborative governance" – meant to reflect shared governance while honouring Indigenous principles of community-based leadership and self-determination. However, the provincial government maintained ultimate authority over child welfare services, including funding. While the government espoused discourses of collaboration that honoured autonomy, self-determination, and accountability, they simultaneously held power over child welfare by "dissociat[ing] itself from responsibilities while sustaining no significant costs regarding its power as ultimate decision-maker" (MacDonald & Levasseur, 2014, p. 108). In other words, the government maintained ultimate power and authority, yet none of the responsibility. The results of these reforms and other policy changes under the New Democratic Party (NDP) government and in the years leading up to our research, 2007–15, meant that the demands on the child welfare service grew, funding did not keep pace with growth, social worker workloads became unmanageable, and children and families were – and remain – underserved (Camfield, 2018).

The Dispossession of Women

The political relevance of gender to the issue of child welfare is also of crucial importance, yet sidelined in both provinces. In 2001, the elimination of the BC Department for Women's Equality led to reductions in the supports available to women who face barriers to participation in the paid labour force (including caregiving responsibilities, disability, and racism); "funding for community-based organizations advocating for, and providing services to, women; and, an exponential increase in unpaid caregiving work, as services are cut back and women take up the slack in their families and communities" (Teghtsoonian, 2003, p. 30). Spending cuts on childcare, for example, amounted to $10 million so that the system could be "more affordable for taxpayers" (p. 30). Funding for forty-seven childcare resource and referral agencies throughout the province were cut to zero in March 2004; thirty-seven community-based women's centres, which provided information, referral, and advocacy services to women, were eliminated entirely; funding to support bridging programs, designed to facilitate transition to employment for women who experienced domestic violence, were eliminated; and finally, wide-ranging cuts to programs and community organizations impeded "women's access to health services, education, housing, disability supports, social assistance benefits, and legal and advocacy services" (Teghtsoonian, 2003, p. 38).

The systematic dispossession and erasure of poor women and their children in British Columbia – many of them Indigenous and people of colour – through such policies marks neoliberalism as "epistemology, economic strategy, and moral code rolled into one" and "the most recent iteration of (settler) colonialism" (Tuck, 2013, p. 325). "[O]lder colonial beliefs, once expressed explicitly, now expressed implicitly, into language and practices which are far more covert about their civilizing mission" ((Bargh, 2007, p. 13–14 in Tuck, 2013, p. 327)). Neoliberalism's insertion of market values and "market-based relationships" (p. 325) into non-market sectors of human activity has made ordinary people and their children "more politically and economically vulnerable, more fully exposed to the dips and turns of the speculative market, and ultimately, more poor" (Tuck, 2013, p. 325). Settler colonialism is not "a fixed event in time, but a structure that continues to contour the lives of Indigenous people, settlers, and all other subjects of the settler colonial nation-state" (p. 325).

Education Funding

Beyond the impact of social policies previously outlined, both Manitoba and British Columbia have cut expenditures on education, increased institutional controls, and injected excessive amounts of public resources into apparently inefficient, regulatory bureaucracies.

In Manitoba, from 1999 to 2016 and under the New Democratic Party (NDP) government, school funding increases were generally set at or above provincial economic growth and were somewhat reflective of social welfare agendas of the left-leaning government (Yoon, Young & Livingston, 2020). Since 2016, when the Progressive Conservative (PC) government was elected (and then re-elected in 2019), there has been greater imposition of fiscal conservative policy, including limited increases in public school funding, restricted local taxation increases (property tax contributed about 35 per cent of the school system's annual budget), limited wage increases in the public sector, and attempted to undermine collective bargaining.

While the Manitoba government made funding cuts to the public system, there was a gradual increase in the numbers of international students, which has become a growing revenue stream, having the most year-over-year growth proportionately nationally (along with Ontario) (Trilokekar & Tamtik, 2020). Although the internationalization of education in Manitoba began with a learning and cultural focus, it has since become an economic effort (Elnagar & Young, 2021). It is telling that the internationalization of education is situated within the government structure as part of the provincial trade industry portfolio.

In Manitoba, the schools of choice policy reflects market model logics and subsequently promotes inequity, reinforces streaming and homogeneity of students, and becomes a form of social class segregation. In other words, the schools of choice policy, which affects school budgets through the per-pupil funding models, "legitimates rather than mitigates educational inequality" (DeWiele & Edgerton, 2016, p. 203). These types of neoliberal policies foster "parentocracy," where parents – acting as consumers valuing individual advancement over the collective good – draw on their economic, social, and cultural capital to individualize programming for children, thereby exacerbating inequalities (DeWiele & Edgerton, 2016).

The story of education funding in British Columbia begins with how government policy, including "structural funding shortfalls; school and programme choice; and market-driven private and public funding mechanisms" (Poole & Fallon, 2015, p. 341), fragmented the public education system and led to increased privatization through diversification of funding sources within the system. Emphasizing fiscal "prudence," Poole and Fallon argue, governments freeze budgets (BC Liberal Party in 2013) or legislate mandated balanced budgets for school districts (BC Liberal Party in 2001) while introducing new initiatives, such as full-day kindergarten, class size and composition arrangements with *no* additional funding to cover these extra costs. As school district revenues consistently lag behind what is needed to support basic delivery of services, the structural funding shortfall has in effect coerced school districts to create private businesses offering high school programs to international students, opening and running accredited schools overseas, marketing curricula and software, and providing online educational services in foreign countries (e.g., Maple Bear Schools). In 2011–12, West Vancouver school district, serving an affluent community in a highly desirable geographical location, generated $9.8 million in private funding, of which 87 per cent came from international student tuition (Poole & Fallon, 2015).

The dominant narrative of public education in Canada positions policies and reforms as being socially just when they actually serve a broader social policy agenda that is patriarchal, capitalist, and racist (de Saxe, Bucknovitz & Mahoney-Mosedale, 2020). Reduced funding of social and educational services creates miserable conditions for teaching: it increases demands on educators, making it more difficult to provide necessary and equitable supports for their students, particularly those with the greatest needs – those who experience poverty, intergenerational trauma, and marginalization due to ability or language proficiency. The teachers' stories in this volume bear witness to the everyday encounters with children and youth who remain disadvantaged within the education system and relegated to the margins of society's responsibility.

Chapter Overviews

Throughout this study, we have been struck by the efforts made by long-serving and deeply committed teachers – good teachers, if you will – to teach with moral integrity while continuously considering the question of whether they should leave or stay in the profession. The question of leaving or staying is not just any question teachers are dealing with but a profound moral question about how one ought to live as an educator. At the core of leading a good and faithful life is the challenge of responding to the needs and suffering of others, a given in a human life. However, "[f]idelity to oneself is not for the fainthearted" (Lear, 2011, p. 5); this is especially so for teachers given the contemporary dominance of ideologies of the market and managerialism (Ball, 2003). The question of how one should live as a teacher within such miserable conditions involves an ongoing quest for meaning and significance.

In the following chapters we explore teachers' experience and foreground the emotionality that characterizes teachers' ethical obligation especially when their values conflict with those of colleagues, parents, and institutional policy. We draw on the stories that teachers shared with us to illustrate and to reflect upon the following dimensions of ethical obligation: valuing students' singularity (chapter 1), appreciating proximity and cultivating closeness in student–teacher relations (chapter 2), honouring human worth (chapter 3), preserving student dignity (chapter 4), and acknowledging the impossibility of the teacher's desire to live ethically (chapter 5).

Chapter 1, *Precarious Others: Valuing Singularity*, presents the pivotal challenge of obligation to recognize and protect the child's singularity despite a culture of labels, test scores, and grades. Torn between the school district's demand "to know where kids are *at*" and the teacher's wish "to respond to what these kids need and to who they *are*," the teacher feels morally compromised. The teacher reveals that, "I didn't believe that what I was doing was right. I wasn't able to be present to them.... I was treating these children like objects – and I felt complicit ... so I resigned." Here, we enlist Judith Butler's (2010) concept of "framing" – an operation of power that determines the recognizability of others and the precarity of those deemed unrecognizable – to show the ways in which education's most vulnerable children become unrecognizable within a system that is supposedly designed to welcome and serve them. That is, children's precarity is magnified through the persistent and pervasive categorizing, identifying, labelling, psychologizing, and pathologizing that further marginalizes them. Because "the precarity of life imposes an obligation on us" (p. 2), we see in these teachers, their attempts to apprehend the precarious Other beyond the frames of recognition. Thus, in cultivating ethical relationships – particularly with our most precarious children – teachers exhibit a tolerance for doubt and uncertainty, openness to the differences of the Other (signaling a radical alterity), and a willingness to expose their own vulnerabilities.

Chapter 2, *Alienation and Exclusion: Appreciating Proximity,* considers the matrix of professional relations in which teachers work and examines how those relations both support and obstruct teachers' "ethical seeing" (Oliver, 2015, p. 482) of each student. Animated by an understanding of obligation as a promissory relation, teachers recount their efforts "to keep their promises" to recognize the different cultural and historical circumstances in which students grow up, to be openly receptive, and to create "moments of relationality that resist codification" (Todd, 2003, p. 9). However, the achievement of a necessary intimate proximity – an attentiveness to a student's uniqueness before calculation or judgment – may require a teacher cutting herself off from the complex relational dynamics that exists among teachers and other professionals. The sea of obligation, represented by the life of a suicidal seven-year-old child, in which the teacher is immersed, threatens to overwhelm the teacher unless she resists the demands of colleagues to be collaborative and collegial. Paradoxically, she must opt for "a relation of relationlessness" (Clarke & Phelan, 2017, p. 21) that excludes specialists (such as psychologists and social workers) and must marginalize herself in order to cultivate a relationship with the child, build her capacity to face up to his reality alongside him, and to tolerate the professional and personal risk in doing so.

Chapter 3, *Shamed and Shaming: Honouring Students,* pursues the teacher's obligation to minimize harm by appreciating and preserving the worth of each student. Historically, schools have been contoured by shame – a crucial mechanism of normalization. The preoccupation with achievement and the circulation of objects such as report cards and academic awards leaves "a lingering feeling of impotence" (Caputo, 1993, p. 349) and humiliation for many teachers, students, and even parents. Needless suffering abounds. Report card time and award events heighten the teacher's sense of wrongdoing. Agonizing over the detrimental role evaluation played in her school, one teacher described the shame of students who felt they were "stupid" while their parents "worship[ped] at the altar of the report card." As a result, the teacher spent a lot of time trying to remedy her students' "lack of belief in themselves" while fearing further public shaming when her own "pedagogies fall right apart." To minimize harm to others is, for Caputo, to recognize and bear witness to those who experience shame. Drawing on Silvan Tomkins's (1984) theorizing of affect and Elspeth Probyn's (2004) in-depth study of shame, we examine the nexus of shame and obligation and ask whether it is possible to de-pathologize shame so that it might be seen as a resource for imagining less restrictive and less fatalistic forms of educational life.

Chapter 4, *Destitute and Dying: Preserving Dignity*, examines the teacher's obligation to uphold the dignity of her students and to guard against any form of exploitation (van Manen, 2012). We ask, what is the teacher's obligation to care for the "one who has been laid low, to victims and outcasts" and to alleviate suffering wherever possible? (Caputo, 1993, p. 145). One teacher tells the story of a student's sudden death on the playground, while a school counsellor tells of a young man's suicide attempt and his subsequent homelessness. Another tells the unlikely story of an international, homestay student who suffers physical and emotional neglect by her host family. In the face of poverty, death, and deprivation, we argue that the obligation to care is inherently a form of madness and "excessive inclination" on the part of teachers (Jung, 2015, p. 62). Care in such situations is eccentric, foolish even, requiring that teachers work in the worst schools, labouring on behalf of students who have been abandoned or neglected or who are suffering. To preserve the dignity of the Other may require that teachers live their lives "in the lowercase" (Caputo, 1993, p. 145), that is, with humility and without recognition for their efforts.

In chapter 5, *Fears and Frustrations: Acknowledging Desire* we take up the burden of obligation as reflecting an impossible desire. When cast in terms of obligation, teaching demands too much of the teacher; she is in danger of being consumed, annihilated by the frustration and fears of not being able to respond to the incessant demands of obligation to the Other. As one teacher expressed it: "physically and mentally I have nothing left to give." The bad dreams of failing to meet one's obligations are, in effect, what Freud would call a "typical dream." The so-called typical dream reflects three affective conflicts, specifically "the burden of responsibility, the worry of failing to meet this responsibility and the expectation of and need for punishment"

(Britzman, 2006, p. 136). The teacher's impossible desire to honour her obligations represents the "the tragedy of everyday life" (Phillips, 2012, p. 33), where everyone is left wanting – each player harbouring desires impossible for the other to fulfil: the students need more, the parents want the impossible, the public expects everything, and the teacher fails to meet her own desire. We explore the ways in which the teacher's fears and frustrations are not a weakness that can be overcome, but rather reflect the teacher's human existence and are the experiences of the good-enough teacher. The good-enough teacher is one who can tolerate the uncertainty – and inevitable frustration – one faces in responding to the call of obligation.

In chapter 6, *Revitalizing Teaching as Vocation*, we consider the notion of vocation as a way of reclaiming the importance of ethical obligation in teaching. Preceding chapters attest to the destructive inclinations imminent in education (categorization and ranking of students) as well as those exaggerated by neoliberalism (reproduction of inequity and heightened accountability). The concept of vocation, as a response to a calling that reflects a particular ethos, may play a crucial role in rescuing education and teaching from some of those toxic tendencies. Repeatedly, teachers in our study shared their aspirations to value the singularity, honour the worth, and preserve the dignity of each student. Their stories attest to how such substantive values are in danger of disappearing altogether in educational institutions "ordered by rationalization, bureaucracy and capitalism" (Brown, 2017, p. 63). Their experiences reflect the fragility of teaching as "a calling [that] ceases to be a calling when it becomes a means to some other end" (Brown, 2017, p. 84). That said, teachers' stories attest to their commitment, resolve, and trust in a future yet to come. So, while without vocation teaching risks becoming meaningless, vocations are always set in contexts within which one must comply *and* resist. The classroom is not simply a space but a place that is "not only physical, but cultural, often spiritual and certainly historical" (Pinar, 2019, p. 19), and always political. In the face of obligation, however, "the upside of [the teacher's] anxiety" (Ruti, 2014, p. 141) is that it provokes and sustains the teacher's own singularity as an ethical subject – her irreplaceability and inimitability – summoning her beyond complacency towards response.

Our representation of teachers' stories in this volume signals our commitment to bring them to the attention of readers so that like these teachers we too can become witnesses who are responsive and accountable. Together, we hope, teachers and researchers testify to a shared history of concerns about what teaching does to teachers in these neoliberal times.

References

Badiou, A. (2014). *Infinite thought: Truth and the return to philosophy*. London/ New York. Bloomsbury Academic.

Ball, S. (2003). The risks of social reproduction: The middle class and education markets. *London Review of Education, 1*(3), 163–75. https://doi.org/10.1080/1474846032000146730

Bargh, M. (Ed.). (2007). *Resistance: An Indigenous response to neoliberalism*. Huia.

Benhabib, S. (2003). *The reluctant modernism of Hannah Arendt*. Rowman & Littlefield.

Blackstock, C. (2007). Residential schools: Did they really close or just morph into child welfare? *Indigenous Law Journal, 6*(1), 71–8.

Britzman, D.P. (2006). *Novel education: Psychoanalytic studies of learning and not learning*. Peter Lang.

Brown, W. (1995). *States of injury: Power and freedom in late modernity*. Princeton University Press.

– (2015a). *Undoing the demos: Neoliberalism's stealth revolution*. Zone Books.

– (2015b). Booked #3: What exactly is neoliberalism? Interview. *Dissent*. https://www.dissentmagazine.org/blog/booked-3-what-exactly-is-neoliberalism-wendy-brown-undoing-the-demos

– (2017). The vocation of the public university. In A.B. Jørgensen, J.J. Justesen, N. Bech, N. Nykrog, & R.B. Clemmensen (Eds.), *What is education? An anthology on education* (pp. 55–89). Problema.

Butler, J. (2010). *Frames of war: When is life grievable?* Verso Books.

Camfield, D. (2018). Manitoba: Fiscal policy and the public sector under "Today's NDP." In B.M. Evans & C. Fanelli (Eds.), *The public sector in an age of austerity: Perspectives from Canada's provinces and territories* (pp. 101–38), McGill-Queen's Press.

Caputo, J.D. (1993). *Against ethics: Contributions to a poetics of obligation with constant reference to deconstruction*. Indiana University Press.

– (2012). Teaching the event: Deconstruction, hauntology, and the scene of pedagogy. *Philosophy of Education Archive*, 23–34. https://doi.org/10.47925/2012.023

Carpenter, S., Weber, N., & Schugurensky, D. (2012). Views from the blackboard: Neoliberal education reforms and the practice of teaching in Ontario, Canada. *Globalisation, Societies and Education, 10*(2), 145–61. https://doi.org/10.1080/14767724.2012.647401

Carson, T. (2017). Title. In M.A. Doll (Ed.), *The reconceptualization of curriculum studies: A Festschrift in honor of William F. Pinar* (pp. 50–8). Routledge.

Clarke, M., & Phelan, A.M. (2017). *Teacher education and the political: The power of negative thinking*. Routledge.

Cochran-Smith, M., Villegas, A.M., Abrams, L. We., Chavez-Moreno, L.C., Mills, T., & Stern, R. (2016). Research on teacher preparation: Charting the landscape of a sprawling field. In D. Gitomer & C.A. Bell (Eds.), *Handbook of research on teaching* (5th Ed.), (pp. 439–548).

Conle, C. (1999). Why narrative? Which narrative? Struggling with time and place in life and research. *Curriculum Inquiry, 29*(1), 7–32. https://doi.org/10.1111/0362-6784.00111

Crocco, M.S., & Costigan, A.T. (2007). The narrowing of curriculum and pedagogy in the age of accountability urban educators speak out. *Urban Education, 42*(6), 512–35. https://doi.org/10.1177/0042085907304964

de Boer, K., Rothwell, D., & Lee, C. (2013). *Child and family poverty in Canada: Implications for child welfare research* (Information Sheet 123E). Canadian Child Welfare Research Portal. Centre for Research on Children and Families, McGill University. https://cwrp.ca/publications/child-and-family-poverty-canada-implications-child-welfare-research

de Saxe, J.G., Bucknovitz, S., & Mahoney-Mosedale, F. (2020). The deprofessionalization of educators: An intersectional analysis of neoliberalism and education "reform." *Education and Urban Society, 52*(1), 51–69. https://doi.org/10.1177/0013124518786398

DeWiele, C.E.B., & Edgerton, J.D. (2016). Parentocracy revisited: Still a relevant concept for understanding middle class educational advantage? *Interchange, 47*(2), 189–210. https://doi.org/10.1007/s10780-015-9261-7

Elnagar, A., & Young, J. (2021). International education and the internationalization of public schooling in Canada: Approaches and conceptualizations. *Canadian Journal of Educational Administration and Policy/ Revue Canadienne en Administration et Politique de l'Éducation, 195*, 80–94. https://doi.org/10.7202/1075674ar

First Call British Columbia Child and Youth Advocacy Coalition. (2020). 2020 BC Poverty Report Card. Accessed on July 31 at: https://still1in5.ca/

Frankel, S. (2012). Poverty reduction in Manitoba under neoliberalism: Is the third way an effective way? *Manitoba Law Journal, 36*, 269.

General Child and Family Services Authority. *Authority History*. Retrieved from https://generalauthority.ca

Hansen, D. (2017). Bearing witness to teaching and teachers. *Journal of Curriculum Studies, 49*(1), 7–23. https://doi.org/10.1080/00220272.2016.1205137

– (2021). *Reimagining the call to teach: A witness to teachers and teaching*. Teachers College Press.

Hansen, D. T., & Sullivan, R. (2022). What renders a witness trustworthy? Ethical and curriculum notes on a mode of educational inquiry. *Studies in Philosophy and Education, 41*, 141–72. https://doi.org/10.1007/s11217-021-09800-w

Hood, C. (1991). A public management for all seasons? *Public Administration, 69*, 3–19. https://doi.org/10.1111/j.1467-9299.1991.tb00779.x

Hyneman Knight, F. (2017). *The ethics of competition*. Routledge.
Jeannotte, M.S. (2010). Going with the flow: Neoliberalism and cultural policy in Manitoba and Saskatchewan. *Canadian Journal of Communication, 35*(2). https://doi.org/10.22230/cjc.2010v35n2a2184
Jung, J.H. (February 2015). *Self-care and care-for-others in education*. [Unpublished doctoral dissertation], The University of British Columbia, Vancouver, Canada.
Laitsch, D. (2013). Smacked by the invisible hand: The wrong debate at the wrong time with the wrong people. *Journal of Curriculum Studies, 45*(1), 16–27. https://doi.org/10.1080/00220272.2012.754948
Lear, J. (2011). *A case for irony*. Harvard University Press.
MacDonald, F., & Levasseur, K. (2014). Accountability insights from the devolution of Indigenous child welfare in Manitoba. *Canadian Public Administration, 57*(1), 97–117. https://doi.org/10.1111/capa.12052
MacIntyre, A.C. (1984). *After virtue. A study in moral theory*. Notre Dame: University of Notre Dame Press.
Mayer, D., Goodwin, A.L., & Mockler, N. (2021). Teacher education policy: Future research, teaching in contexts of super-diversity and early career teaching. In D. Mayer (Ed.), *Teacher education policy and research: Global perspectives*, (pp. 209–23). Springer.
McBride, S., & McNutt, K. (2007). Devolution and neoliberalism in the Canadian welfare state. *Global Social Policy*, 7(2), 177–201. https://doi.org/10.1177/1468018107078161
Moore, M., & Slee, R. (2020). Disability studies, inclusive education and exclusion. In N. Watson & S. Vehmas (Eds.), *Routledge handbook of disability studies* (2nd ed., pp. 265–80). Routledge.
Oliver, K. (2001). *Witnessing: Beyond recognition*. University of Minnesota Press.
– (2015). Witnessing, recognition, and response ethics. *Philosophy and Rhetoric, 48*(4), 473–93. https://doi.org/10.5325/philrhet.48.4.0473
Organisation of Economic Co-operation and Development. (2019). TALIS 2018 results (Volume 1): Teachers and school leaders as lifelong learners. TALIS, OECD Publishing, Paris. http://doi.org/10.1787/1d0bc92a-en
Pacini-Ketchabaw, V. (2021). Witnessing encounters: A response to Nicole Ineese-Nash's "Ontologies of Welcoming." Bank Street Occasional Paper Series, 45(5). Retrieved from http://educate.bankstreet.edu/occasional-paper-series/
Parker, L. (2017). Creating a crisis: Selling neoliberal policy through the rebranding of education. *Canadian Journal of Educational Administration and Policy*, 183, 44–60.
Phelan, A.M., & Rüsselbaek Hansen, D. (2018). Reclaiming agency and appreciating limits in teacher education: Existential, ethical, and psychoanalytical readings. *McGill Journal of Education, 53*(1), 128–45. https://doi.org/10.7202/1056286ar

Phillips, A. (2012). *Missing out: In praise of the unlived life*. Picador.

Pinar, W.F. (2019). *Moving images of eternity: George Grant's critique of time, teaching, and technology*. The University of Ottawa Press.

Pitt, A., & Britzman, D. (2003). Speculations on qualities of difficult knowledge in teaching and learning: An experiment in psychoanalytic research. *Qualitative Studies in Education, 16*(6), 755–76. https://doi.org/10.1080/09518390310001632135

Polkinghorn, D. (1988). *Narrative knowing and the human sciences*. State University of New York Press.

Poole, W., & Fallon, G. (2015). The emerging fourth tier in K–12 education finance in British Columbia, Canada: Increasing privatisation and implications for social justice. *Globalisation, Societies and Education, 13*(3), 339–68. https://doi.org/10.1080/14767724.2014.996857

Probyn, E. (2004). Teaching bodies: Affects in the classroom. *Body & Society, 10*(4), 21–43. https://doi.org/10.1177/1357034x04047854

Rogan, Ann I., & de Kock, D.M. (2005). Chronicles from the classroom: Making sense of the methodology and methods of narrative analysis. *Qualitative Inquiry, 11*(4), 628–49. https://doi.org/10.1177/1077800405276777

Ruti, M. (2014). *The call of character: Living a life worth living*. Columbia University Press.

Schaefer, L., Long, J.S., & Clandinin, D.J. (2012). Questioning the research on early career teacher attrition and retention. *Alberta Journal of Educational Research, 58*(1), 106–21.

Schiff, J.L. (2014). *Burdens of political responsibility: Narrative and cultivation of responsiveness*. Cambridge University Press.

Schwandt, T. (2003). Three epistemological stances for qualitative inquiry: Interpretivism, hermeneutics, and social constructivism. In N.K. Denzin & Y.S. Lincoln (Eds.), *The landscape of qualitative research: Theories and issues*, (2nd ed., pp. 292–331). Sage.

Scott, C.E. (1995). Caputo on obligation without origin: Discussion of against ethics. *Research in Phenomenology, 25*(1), 249–60. https://doi.org/10.1163/156916495x00149

Social Planning Council of Winnipeg (2020). Broken promises, stolen futures: Child and family poverty in Manitoba. Manitoba Report Card 2020. www.spcw.mb.ca

Stack, M. (2006). Testing, testing, read all about it: Canadian press coverage of the PISA results. *Canadian Journal of Education, 29*(1), 49–69. https://doi.org/10.2307/20054146

Teghtsoonian, K. (2003). W(h)ither women's equality? Neoliberalism, institutional change and public policy in British Columbia. *Policy and Society, 22*(1), 26–47. https://doi.org/10.1016/s1449-4035(03)70012-5

Todd, S. (2003). *Learning from the other: Levinas, psychoanalysis, and ethical possibilities in education*. The State University of New York Press.

Tomkins, S.S. (1984). Affect theory. *Approaches to emotion, 163*(163–95).

Trilokekar, R.D., & Tamtik, M. (2020). A comparative analysis of the K–12 international education policies of Ontario and Manitoba. *Canadian Journal of Educational Administration and Policy*, 193, 32–48.

Tuck, E. (2013). Neoliberalism as nihilism? A commentary on educational accountability, teacher education, and school reform. *Journal for Critical Education Policy Studies, 11*(2), 324–47.

van Manen, M. (2012). The call of pedagogy as the call of contact. *Phenomenology & Practice, 6*(2), 8–34. https://doi.org/10.29173/pandpr19859

Wotherspoon, T. (2020). Schools as "really dangerous places" for Indigenous children and youth: Schools, child welfare, and contemporary challenges to reconciliation. *The Canadian Review of Sociology (La Revue Canadienne de Sociologie), 57*(1), 34–52. https://doi.org/10.1111/cars.12267. Medline:32011084

Yoon, E.-S., Young, J., & Livingston, E. (2020). From bake sales to million-dollar school fundraising campaigns: The new inequity. *Journal of Educational Administration and History, 52*(1), 25–38. https://doi.org/10.1080/00220620.2019.1685473

Chapter 1

Precarious Others: Valuing Singularity

I was constantly overwhelmed by the assessments. I didn't believe in it philosophically and, honestly, sometimes it felt more like the district was assessing me. It was ridiculous – I just wanted to spend time being with the kids. And so I was just done.

– Faye, elementary school teacher

In the current neoliberal era, large-scale assessments are implemented as a means to measure the education system's effectiveness, rank performances (of countries, districts, and students), and quantify students' skills and knowledge. Aside from globally produced tests, there has also been a move in some school districts to create and implement large-scale assessments locally. Yet, large-scale assessments – with their preoccupations with quantifying, measuring, comparing, and ranking – diminish teachers' capacities to respond ethically to children. Testing takes priority over teaching. Faye's narrative illustrates the ways in which her attempts to build relationships with children were undermined by the system's incessant desire to know students through testing them, frustrating Faye and culminating in her early departure from the profession. Sadly, Faye's narrative is similar to many stories we heard during our interviews with teachers and is reflective of an education system rooted in Kantian conceptions of static knowledge, which is determined to *know* children. The responsibility for this education agenda based on knowledge accumulation of children and knowledge transfer of curriculum is borne by teachers who are expected to know the curriculum and children in contracted ways. In turn, children are expected to be passive objects of assessment, intervention, and improvement according to generalized and arbitrary standards rooted in Euro-Western epistemologies. When education's epistemological foundations are based on technical discursive regimes seeking to *know* children, teachers' capacities to read and respond to the differences or "otherness" of the children who present themselves in schools is diminished. The violence of seeking standardization and turning "otherness" into sameness is amplified in the current neoliberal climate of increased managerialism and accountability, eroding spaces for the teacher's judgment, responsiveness, and relationships, and affecting the subjectivities of both the teacher and the student.

Our purpose in this chapter is to centre the emotionality of teachers' obligations to children as precarious Others, and to consider the tensions teachers experience within educational systems that valorize technocratic conceptions of knowledge, teachers, and students. We will illustrate the effects that education's technocratic efforts to *know* children have on teachers' subjectivities and consider the ways in which discourses that privilege knowledge construct the teacher as expert (the one who must *know*) and concomitantly construct the child as object (the one to *be known*). Then, we will enlist Judith Butler's (2010) work on framing – an operation of power that determines the recognizability of others and the precarity of those deemed unrecognizable – to consider the ways in which education's most vulnerable children become unrecognizable within a system that should be designed to serve them. That is, their precarity is magnified through the persistent and pervasive categorizing, identifying, labelling, psychologizing, and pathologizing that further marginalizes them. Because "the precarity of life imposes an obligation on us" (Butler, 2010, p. 2), we see in these teachers their attempts to apprehend the precarious Other beyond the frames of recognition. Thus, in cultivating ethical relationships – particularly with society's most precarious children – teachers exhibit a tolerance for doubt and uncertainty, an openness to the differences of the Other, and a willingness to expose their own vulnerabilities. Here we will explore the qualities of teachers' ethical relations with their students, marked by their commitments to learn from the Other through the preservation of the child's alterity, engagements with curiosity, and tolerance for uncertainty.

Schooling as Mastery *over* the Other

The project of schooling is premised on particular epistemologies. Traditionally, schools have been transmitters of knowledge (via the sanctioned curriculum) but also generators of knowledge – mining bits of knowledge about students from test scores, inventories, and norms; assessing and measuring students; and then sorting and categorizing them. When the knowledge generated indicates that students do not measure up, the education system also presumes to know how to intervene; imposing remedies to fix, catch up, remediate, close the gap, segregate, or discipline the learner. These processes reflect the education system's reverence for knowledge that is authorized, objective, fixed, and void of context, revealing education's "institutionalized fantasy of mastery" (Butler, 2004, p. 29). An epistemology of mastery is a discursive regime of truth – infusing, constructing, and reifying all aspects of schooling. Within this discourse that privileges mastery, teachers are required to be masters of curriculum and of children, and children are expected to master what is taught.

Discourses of mastery have both epistemological and ontological implications. Epistemologically, the curriculum becomes a tool of knowledge transmission rather than a pedagogical site of knowledge co-creation and transformation. Whereas, ontologically, the implicitly power-laden and hierarchical teacher–student relationship, premised on knowledge transmission and knowing the Other, constitutes and reiterates particular teacher and student subjectivities. The teacher becomes responsible for transmitting and assessing seemingly neutral knowledge; and the children – like objects – become sorted, identified, categorized, and disciplined according to their capacities to acquire the standardized knowledge. Importantly, when the teacher–student relationship is premised on the requirement of *knowing* the Other – a mastery of the teacher over the student – it undermines the complexities of attending and responding ethically to the complicated lives of children, creating tension for the teacher between the prescribed ways of teaching and her sense of obligation to the student. Therefore, to seek to *know* the Other is a rational – not relational – view of the Other and constitutes the subjectivity of the teaching subject as *expert*, responsible for knowing curriculum and the child, while framing the child as one who is defined by standards and deviations from them.

Teacher as Expert

The Latin meaning of obligation is "to bind" and illustrates the seemingly physical sense of obligation as that of being tied to the Other through promise or duty. To respond to the Other requires that teachers are receptive to the disruptions by the Other (a child's questions, outbursts, or tears), and subsequently means that the teachers are open to the undecidability of how to respond to the Other, remaining uncertain in their judgments (Janzen & Phelan, 2018). Yet, education's epistemological presuppositions of *knowing* the child have ontological effects. That is, education's desire to know charges the teacher not just with defining *what* the child knows, but also with determining *who* the child is and can be. There is an assumption that if the teacher knows the child and knows about the child – her background and broader experiences – that the teacher will be better equipped to teach the child (Todd, 2003). These discourses of *knowing* create a "teacher as expert" discourse that subjugates the teacher – an identity subjected and constituted by discourses that come before the teacher (Butler, 1997; Davies, 2006). As Butler (1997) theorizes, subjection is "the process of becoming subordinated by power as well as the process of becoming a subject" (p. 2); both dominated but also activated or formed as the subject. In other words, "what I can 'be,' is constrained in advance by a regime of truth that decides what will and will not be a recognizable form of being" (Butler, 2005, p. 22). The teaching subject then, discursively determined as expert, requires compliance with the particular norms that precede it. Thus, the teacher's identity becomes framed in such a way that, as expert, the teacher's sense of obligation to the Other is undermined in that the *uncertainty* required in responding ethically is not a recognizable form of being the teaching subject. As expert, the teaching subject's ability to be uncertain and undecided is constricted; in her obligation to respond to the child, she experiences an ontological tension between being recognizable as teacher (as expert) and responding ethically (with uncertainty and undecidability) in the face of the Other.

Consider Michelle, an elementary teacher of eight years and teaching grade six in an urban school, who described herself as "feeling pretty confident with knowing the curriculum and understanding children of this particular age group" and as "having a really good rapport with families." Yet, Michelle also described feeling incredible pressure for implementing the district's prescribed math and reading programs and the additional district-imposed large-scale assessments. She explained: "We have to do all of this online reporting to the district – *on top of* report cards. We could save ourselves a whole lot of work here and use our professional judgment instead of filling in all these forms. But that's not what we are supposed to be doing. If we got audited for our assessment stuff, right, like we could be in trouble if we don't have documentation to back it up." Michelle complained that the prescribed approaches "don't align with my beliefs" and that they diminished her "freedom to teach." Yet, Michelle's ability to be recognizable as a teacher is dependent on her performance as expert, a form of being decided in advance (Butler, 2005). Thus, for Michelle to be recognizable as a "teacher," she must comply with the narratives in which implementing assessment protocols are prescribed and valued over her professional judgment. These expert discourses of the teacher precede her, authorizing an identity that requires her to "know" children through predetermined and standardized assessments.

Additionally, Michelle explained that part of her recognizability as a competent teacher carries the enormous weight of being judged by her colleagues, the school's parents, and the district administrators. She described colleagues questioning her if she left the school before five o'clock at night, insinuating that she had likely not completed her work. She worried about "the parents [who] are out front of the school watching from their cars." Michelle scorned the incessant surveillance, stating that she felt as though "Big Brother is always watching." She explained, "They have a lot of power. I could be fired if they're not happy with the way I'm doing things." Michelle attempted to shore up her confidence and demonstrate her competence as a teacher by doing schoolwork (planning and marking) every night and on weekends so that she "can be prepared," and hopefully, avoid being so harshly judged. Under constant scrutiny, she tried to alleviate her worries that people would think that she was "not doing as much" as she could be.

Ball (2003) reminds us that in the current educational era of standardization and accountability, these technologies of managerialism prescribe the teacher's performativity. As Ball explains, "performativity is a technology, a culture and a mode of regulation … [where teachers'] performances (of individual subjects or organizations) serve as measures of productivity or output, or displays of 'quality'" (p. 216). Thus, the performativity of the teaching subject comes to represent what is valued within the system, "where commitment, judgement and authenticity within practice are sacrificed for impression and performance" (Ball, 2003, p. 221). Because of the increased surveillance and constant judgment, where outputs represent what is worthwhile, we see the ways in which Michelle was required to perform "teacher" in particular ways. Thus, the teaching subject becomes regulated through technologies of surveillance, shifting teachers' attention from people to performance and from students to standards.

The teaching subject is also regulated through the internalization of discourses of surveillance. That is, although Michelle opposed the imposed programming and testing, as well as the heightened district demands of accountability, she had (unwittingly) internalized these regulatory discourses. For example, when the principal told Michelle to use her judgment on some of the assessments, encouraging her to complete the forms based on her previous knowledge of the child, Michelle worried about being "audited" and then "getting in trouble for not have the documentation to back up" the students' scores. The demands and discourses of the oppressive testing regimes seemed to create a sense of distrust of her own knowledge of the child and manifest in a perpetual sense of "second-guessing myself." She even reinforces the implicit suspicions of her professional judgment, stating, "Are you kidding me!? We went to all this in-servicing. Millions of dollars were probably spent on this and now you're saying, 'Use your professional judgement.'" While on the one hand, Michelle saw the large-scale assessments as problematic and as interfering with her own beliefs about teaching and with her relationships with children; on the other hand, she regulated her own judgment, complying with the demands imposed out of fear, thereby illustrating the ways in which these expert discourses regulate the performativity of the teaching subject.

Michelle's narratives illustrate the ways expert discourses – through incessant regulation and surveillance – threaten the teacher who might not do, know, or be enough. Teachers' performativity is a compliance with the constant – and often implicit – demands; the late-night planning seeking to fulfil the fantasy of the perfectly planned and executed lesson, the continual testing and tracking of progress, the marking and reporting that seeks to sort and identify students' transgressions from the predetermined trajectory, and the complying with the expectations of the accumulative and regulatory gaze of others. Expert discourses, regulated through technologies of surveillance, come to bear on the teacher's subjectivity – who and how she is allowed to be – and help to illuminate what teaching does to teachers. Teachers, like Michelle, feel torn between wanting to teach with a sense of moral integrity and complying with the normative discourses of expert that precede her. Michelle, although only in her early thirties, complained about being "emotionally exhausted and constantly stressed." She said, "I can't take a sick day. I just drag myself out of bed. I constantly feel like I need to be giving more." But what more can she give? Michelle did not say. The incessant surveillance she experienced created a sense of needing to do teaching right, while at the same time reducing what is right about teaching.

Child as Object

The hierarchically dominant teacher seeking recognizability as expert is subsequently expected to have expert knowledge about the child – to *know* the student in particular ways. Enlisting large-scale tools of evaluation and assessment, teachers are required to determine what knowledge the child has or has acquired in order to determine in what regard – and to what extent – the child is deficient. As Sharon Todd (2003) reminds us, to assume to *know* the Other induces a violent erasure of the particularities and differences of the Other – where the Other becomes reduced to norms. Further, to know the Other presumes both that the Other *can* be known and also that this is a pedagogical and ethical endeavour in the first place (Todd, 2003). Such assumptions devalue the Other, diminishing the ethical relations between the teacher and the child – a relationship that requires the teacher's questioning, indecision, and judgment. When the teacher is supposed to *know* the Other in particular ways, she must collect and collate that information in order to determine the child, reducing the child to an object, void of context and subjectivity. Faye, who was a teacher for sixteen years, became so disenchanted with her school district's mandatory testing regime that she resigned from teaching: "It's tough because I had to judge my students, and yet, I didn't feel like what I was doing was right. I was in the trap because I didn't want it to be this way, and yet I had to be. The district had us create this snowball of papers and reports and it all took so much time. Then it all got filed – which was ridiculous because we didn't have anywhere to keep it, and no one ever read it anyway! And then, in grade seven, the kids leave the school and it all got tossed – shredded." The educational system's requirement to *know* the child operates discursively through language while also inscribing language, pedagogies, policies, and practices, manifesting materially in benchmarks, outcomes, standards, and other measurement regimes. The time-consuming demands of the constant evaluating and testing of students, the subsequent administrative task of collecting and compiling the data, the enormous "paper trail" that was created, and the files that were compiled illustrate the assumptions that the education system makes about the knowability of the students. It has a dehumanizing effect on children in that they become presumably "known" through – and known *as* – their scores, rankings, and grades.

Like Michelle, Faye described the frustrations she felt in participating in the school district's effort to *know* children through the large-scale testing as an onerous and time-consuming process, objectifying children and minimizing teachers' relationships with them. Faye explained her frustration: "The district wanted to know where kids are *at*, but we need to respond to what these kids need and to who they *are*." We see in Faye's account the tension she experienced in being compelled to do something that diminished her obligation to respond ethically to her students, foregrounding the difference between a rational and relational way of being with children (Todd, 2003). Faye said: "We've completely lost sight of the kids in all of this! I didn't believe that what I was doing was right. I didn't – I wasn't able to be present with them. I felt awful because I felt like I was treating these children like objects – and I felt complicit. I was not myself. I was not the teacher I wanted to be, and so I resigned." Ultimately, Faye's complicity in doing something that she did not feel was "right" became burdensome and led to her resignation.

As we see with both Michelle and Faye, their experiences of the tensions between the demands of the education system to *know* children and their own sense of obligation *to* children manifested in feelings of guilt, fear, and frustration. The expert discourses inscribe the teaching subject, requiring them to *know* the Other, and have a constitutive and regulatory effect on them. The teaching subject must enact expert as one who knows curriculum (in advance and without destiny) and also as one who *knows* the students (in rational, not relational, ways). In presuming to *know* the Other, a violence is enacted through "shrouding the Other in my totality" (Todd, 2003, p. 215). Stated differently, the Other becomes that which can be claimed by me, becoming "the object of my comprehension, my world, my narrative, reducing the Other to me" (Todd, 2003, p. 15). Therefore, to claim to *know* the Other is a violent subsuming of the Other, an erasure of the Other's difference, and effectively undermines a capacity to share in an ethical relationality with an Other. As with Faye and Michelle, the teacher is regulated to comply with the normative identities of expert in order to be recognizable as a teacher, and, in doing so, end up objectifying children, compromising their relationships with them, and eschewing what they "believed was right." Thus, the teachers described feeling "caught," "trapped," and "complicit;" wedged between a system that constructs – and requires – them to be experts seeking rational *knowledge about* the Other, while at the same time, induces their sense of neglect in responding to their felt obligation to children.

The Child as Precarious

Although an education system premised on *knowing* defines and delineates the teaching subject in particular ways, it also has detrimental effects on the subjectivities of children, already "Othered" and therefore assigned a diminished status. As Cannella (2000) explains, children are "the ultimate 'Other' than the adult – those who must have their decisions made for them because they are not yet mature – those who must gain knowledge that has been legitimized by those who are older and wiser – those whose ways of being in the world can be uncovered through the experimental and observational methods of science – those who can be labeled as gifted, slow, intelligent, or special" (p. 36). Within the education system (and reflective of the larger society in general), children are always deemed lesser, deficient, and knowable, which presumably justifies the surveillance and regulation imposed upon them. The education system's desire for mastery over students frames children in particular ways, reinforcing normalized ideals of the child and then excluding, punishing, and disciplining those who exceed the frames. Frames are politically informed and reflect operations of power, and, according to Butler (2010), "become part of the very practice of ordering and regulating subjects according to pre-established norms" (p. 141). Therefore, frames, while determining who counts as a student, also determine who does not. Frames matter – particularly for those who are deemed precarious, that is, those whose lives are in the hands of others, "a dependency on people we know, or barely know, or know not at all" (Butler, 2010, p. 14). Children are precarious because of their Otherness and their reliance on adults for their safe and healthy existence. Reciprocally, this means that teachers are obligated to these children as their students. Importantly, children with greater social and economic disadvantages and those who demonstrate behavioural non-compliance have exacerbated precarity and are often further scrutinized and marginalized through legal, medical, and psychological discourses (Janzen & Schwartz, 2018). And because frames determine the child's recognizability, the children who are more precarious are at risk of being less recognizable as students – or worse, not recognizable at all. Consider Stacey's account of her time teaching in middle years:

> I had this one boy, Chris.... He was just – he had so many barriers in his life that made it really hard for him to be successful. He had no chance because the teachers before had bad mouthed him and said that "he's never going to amount to anything but a criminal." He hated school and it was an awful situation for him – really bad. So, when he arrived in my class, the other teachers tried to warn me about him, but I just made it my mission to not be that teacher. Instead I wanted to be somebody that Chris would look back on and would know that I loved him – even if he had other horrible experiences in his life. He had so many things working against him, but I saw all of these qualities in him.

We see in Stacey's narrative the ways in which Chris, a boy already Othered because of his status as a child, falls outs of the frame of "student" and so becomes less/unrecognizable by some of the teachers. When students cannot, do not, or will not conform to the frames that determine the student, they become labelled, cast out, and disregarded. The other teachers deemed Chris unrecognizable and determined that "he had no chance." Thus, we see how the frames regulate "which subjects become possible at all or, rather, how they become impossibilities" (Butler, 2010, p. 163). Chris, although only a child, was already an impossibility.

Thomas and Loxley (2007) criticize the authorized – and socially constructed – discourses that frame children as "displaced by a morass of half-understood ideas about disturbance, a jumble of bits and pieces from psychoanalysis, psychology and psychiatry, a bricolage of penis envy and cognitive dissonance, of Freudian slip and standard deviation, of motivation and maternal deprivation, regression and repression, attention seeking and assimilation, reinforcement and self-esteem – ideas corrupted by textbook writers and mangled by journalists and the writers of popular culture" (p. 55). In other words, the means through which education attempts to *know* children is epistemologically, empirically, and ethically fraught, drawing on dissonant disciplines and resulting in superficial and simplistic elucidations of children. As Thomas and Loxley (2007) warn, once children's behaviours become identified as a psychological or social disorder, the need for moral judgment and ethical response is interrupted. The educational purpose morphs from a child's education to the school's need to keep the child in order, illustrating the operations of power at work.

Butler (2004) helps us to understand that "lives are supported and maintained differently.... Certain lives will be highly protected ... [while] other lives will not find such fast and furious support" (p. 32). Chris's precarious existence made him unrecognizable as a student and therefore not worthy of their attention. As with Chris, some children's precarity is magnified by factors of their differences and their deviations from the norms, which exceed the frames of recognizability. Particular social and political conditions in which some children exist – like the numerous barriers of poverty and inequity we see in Chris' situation – exacerbate precarity, making these subjects more vulnerable (Butler, 2004). As Butler (2010) warns, "If certain lives are not considered lives from the start, not conceivable as lives within certain epistemological frames, then these lives are never lived or lost in the fullest sense" (p. 6). Chris, exceeding the frames of recognizability: he is unrecognizable as a student – and as a vulnerable child – by the other teachers. His destiny is already determined: "He won't amount to anything." Left up to the teacher to be seen and acknowledged, while at the same time rendered unrecognizable (Butler, 2010), the child is at risk of not counting in the school's accounting of the child.

The frames that exist within education are the norms by which students' subjectivities are recognized. They are the norms that operate, regulate, and categorize, constituting who is and is not recognizable. At best unnoticed – and at worst, actively ostracized – these students who are already precarious become more vulnerable when they do not measure up. Determined as deviant or deficient by an education epistemology that presumes to *know* them, they are often assumed pre-destined "to end up in jail or dead before he's eighteen," as one of our participants flatly stated. As Butler (2010) explains, "if violence is done against those who are unreal, then, from the perspective of the violence, it fails to injure or negate those lives since those lives are already negated" (p. 33). We can dismiss these children and their futures because these lives are already deemed to be lost (Butler, 2010). Yet, Stacey and Faye sought to *apprehend* – as a mode of knowing or perceiving – the child beyond the frames of recognizability, to acknowledge the child's vulnerability exacerbated by social and political forces (Butler, 2010). They demonstrated a willingness to be in relation with these precarious Others and to engage in the risk of relationality even when these children appeared beyond recognition as students.

Teaching as an Ethical Relation

Many teachers in our study often spoke about the tensions they felt between what the system of education required of them (that is, to *know* the Other through standardized and regulatory means) and their desire for more ethical relations with children, that is, to apprehend children beyond the dominant epistemological and technical frames of schooling. Consider George, a resource teacher in middle school, and his frustrations: "Teaching needs to be more inspirational and more creative and more about the kids. It can't just be about the numbers on the tests." Like Faye and Michelle, George expressed his frustration with the education system's persistent attempts at quantifying children and wished for the valuing of other (not quantifiable) attributes of children, such as creativity and curiosity. In identifying these tensions between rationality and relationality, we see in teachers like George attempts to engage ethically with their students, attempts to *learn from* the Other. These teachers sought to engender an encounter between the self and the Other as a "profoundly ethical event" (Todd, 2003, p. 50) premised on openness and an exposure of one's vulnerability.

But what does it look like to *learn from* the Other? What qualities, dispositions, or practices do teachers enlist in order to enliven such ethical relations with the Other? In responding to these questions, we are reminded of Todd's (2003) distinction between the self and Other. As Todd interprets Levinas, she reminds us that the "encounter between the self and Other is the time and place of responsibility" (p. 50). Although George asserts that teachers need to be focused on rapport and relationship, Todd cautions that these relationships cannot be constituted through pity or sympathy. As Todd explains, "the mystery here is the radical alterity of the Other, and so the encounter must always refuse reducing the Other to a common ground with the self" (p. 51). Thus, although feelings of empathy and sympathy may be important, and even inevitable, an ethical engagement with the Other must maintain the distinction between the self and the Other. In other words, in order to maintain the alterity of the Other – the distinction between the self and the Other – the ethical engagement is not an attempt to seek a common ground, but rather to maintain a divide; to remain attentive and receptive to the differences of the Other (Todd, 2003).

In order to create relationships where difference is valued, one must maintain a disposition of curiosity about and an openness to the Other – resisting knowing the Other through simplistic assumptions and instead being interested in what is *unknown*, what lies beyond the frames of recognition. George relays a story about one particular middle-years student, Brooke:

> The other teachers thought she was lazy. They said, "She's dull." "She's this." "She's that." And her foster parents – she was a kid in care – thought she was a good kid too, but she wasn't their child; so she was good money and wasn't causing trouble for them. So, we have a kid getting low grades and yet no one cared about that – but I think we need to stand up for these kids. That's what we signed up for as teachers. I was fortunate to have the time to just sit with Brooke – to talk with her. It was a chance to work with a kid who was a *mystery* to me.

George resisted the easy and discounting labels of "lazy" and instead wanted to engage with Brooke and to consider the aspects of her that were enigmatic – a mystery to him. We see with George a teaching relation of *learning from* the Other, requiring an openness to the unknown, a disposition of wonder. An ethical relation with the Other requires a resistance to assumptions that the Other can be known and instead a desire to consider the mysteries of and remain curious about the Other. In doing so, one maintains the radical alterity and unknowability of the Other (Todd, 2003).

In maintaining a stance of openness towards the Other, the teacher resists *knowing* or relying on what is *known about* the Other. We see this when George rejects the dismissive descriptors of Brooke, refusing to assume to *know* her as lazy or dull, thereby rejecting the frames that risk making her unrecognizable. George, similar to Stacey, was not satisfied with what was presumed to be known about the student; the rationalized labels that arrive before the child, underscoring the child's precarity and reducing her humanness. Instead, George and Stacey both have a deep interest in *learning from* the student, maintaining an openness to the ambiguity of the Other (Todd, 2003). Here we see that the ethical relation between the teacher and the student, and the ethical possibility of education, as only conceivable when *knowing about* the child (assessing, judging, identifying) is not the objective of the relationship (Todd, 2003). One must be able to resist the rational and limiting labels of education's epistemological hegemony, and rather, cultivate "an eagerness to inquire ... a willingness to suspend judgement and bracket existing – potentially limiting – ways of thinking, seeing, and categorising" (Schinkel, 2017, p. 539). Thus, in order to foster ethical relations and to *learn from* the Other, one must suspend judgments about the Other and attempt to apprehend the child beyond the existing frames of recognizability.

We see the importance of the suspension of judgment in Doug's account of working with a "difficult" high school student, Jeanine. Although Jeanine was "getting by," there was something about her that worried Doug, a high school counsellor. Doug explained, "I spent years developing a relationship with Jeanine. At first she wouldn't even speak to me." According to Doug, Jeanine's other teachers described her as "fairly smart," but they also complained that "she was not a hard worker and rarely did her homework." Doug continued: "One day, she told me everything: her Dad was an alcoholic with terminal cancer who did not live with her and her mom. Her mom was also addicted to alcohol and spent her welfare money on her addiction. Turns out, Jeanine was working three jobs so she could pay the mortgage on the house!" Doug's efforts to develop a relationship with Jeanine took years, and perhaps she finally talked to him simply because he remained open to listening to her. Doug did not seek to *know about* Jeanine, to categorize or diagnose her, and he resisted the dismissive labels assigned by others. Instead, Doug attempted to engage in a relationship with Jeanine without knowing if she would ever even speak with him. The moment of listening illustrated Jeanine's trust in Doug, as well as Doug's tolerance for uncertainty in the listening relationship. In suspending judgment, being patient, and demonstrating openness, Doug eventually earned Jeanine's trust.

In his relationship with Jeanine, Doug was both "passively open and exposed" (Todd, 2004, p. 347) to the alterity of the Other. Put simply, Doug was rendered vulnerable and susceptible to the unforeseen effects of the relationship (Todd, 2003). Doug had helped Jeanine to apply for and receive a $25,000 scholarship for university, and yet this troubled him. He worried about his role in Jeanine's success, vacillating between guilt that perhaps he pushed her to apply for the scholarship and hope that she had an opportunity that she could not have previously imagined. He was pleased for her because "Jeanine was so over the moon happy that she was going to university because no one in her family had even graduated from high school before." Yet, his guilt remained: "I worried that I hadn't done my job correctly." Doug doubted his decisions and worried that Jeanine felt pressure to apply for the scholarships because of his encouragement. These are the risks of ethical relations; when "I am exposed to the Other, I can listen, attend, and be surprised; the Other can affect me" (Todd, 2003, p. 15). Doug was affected by his relationship with Jeanine; affected by his care for her, but also by the concomitant effects of doubt, guilt, and worry. And, like so many of our participants that engaged in these deeply affective relations with the most precarious children, Doug did not know what ever happened to Jeanine.

The Risks of the Ethical Relation

Remaining open to the Other is a risk in that one cannot know in advance what the Other will do or say or what the Other needs or wants. Openness, thus, requires vulnerability and receptiveness to the unforeseeable and unpredictable needs of the Other (Todd, 2003). While the Otherness remains constantly beyond one's grasp, the purpose of being open to the Other is not to come to understand the Other, but rather to "sustain a mode of relation where the love comes into being through response to the Other" (Todd, 2003, p. 89). As we see with Stacey when she declared her decision to simply love Chris, even though she did not even have him as a student yet, she did so as a way of respecting the alterity of the Other. Although her colleagues "warned" her about him, she saw a boy who "no one else seemed to want to spend any time with." Stacey actively rejected her colleagues' stance of presuming to know him as "difficult" and instead, attentive to his precarity and respecting his alterity, Stacey "decided to make it [her] mission to engage, nurture, and love him."

Stacey did not and could not know what would come from her efforts nor did she seem to want anything in return. Her commitment reflected her own vulnerability in the loving relation – her willingness to be uncertain, to be altered, and to risk her own self-assurance (Todd, 2003). Stacey, like Doug, demonstrated a willingness to be open to the unknown and to bear the consequences of the unforeseen effects. According to Todd, it is this continual receptiveness that "ground[s] love's ethical potential" (p. 88). She explains: "This meaning of love therefore suggests that it is not what I know about the Other that is important for establishing connection, but that I simply am for the Other in my feeling for her; I learn from and respond to her difference" (p. 73). These teachers – Stacey, Doug, Faye, and Michelle – simply *are* for the Other: playing on the floor without an ulterior motive, being curious and attentive to their presence, and waiting patiently for a child's story to be revealed. Their engagements with the Other are "not instrumental, not *for* something else" (Schinkel, 2017, p. 549); rather, they are about sustaining an openness to the Other and to the difference of the Other, resolved to cultivate an ethical relationality.

Yet relationships that honour the alterity of Other risk the teachers' own recognizability. In resisting an epistemological imperative to know children, they suspend judgment and maintain their own vulnerability. The teachers' attention to the precarious ones requires their non-compliance with the expert discourses of teaching. As Stacey describes, there was "a lot of pushback from the other teachers, particularly this one staff member. He would not accept that anything positive could happen with Chris." This illustrates how students who are not recognizable within the frames are "cast as threats" (Butler, 2010, p. 31), considered deviant and a danger to the social order of schooling and to society at large. In attempting to engage with the precarious children with openness, Stacey encountered "pushback" and thus risked her own recognizability. In other words, she was contesting the power at work, enacting teacher differently from the norms by rejecting definitive knowledge of the Other.

George's, Doug's, and Stacey's actions illustrate their obligations to the precarious Others, where "something about [their] suffering stops us in our tracks" (Caputo, 1993, p. 32). Their obligations to the Other requires them to act, yet in doing so, they do not enact the teaching subject as prescribed by the discursive norms of knowing. Jeanine and Chris are precarious youth to whom these teachers exposed their own vulnerabilities, to whom they listened without judgment, and to whom they responded without certainty of outcome and without expectation of reciprocity. The teachers demonstrated their willingness to *learn from* children and revealed their own vulnerabilities without an end goal or redemptive tale in mind. Stacey says, in her attempts to engage with Chris, that she "doesn't even know if it made a difference." Yet, Todd (2003) reminds us that, "the point is we can never figure out completely; we cannot calculate, in some algorithmic fashion, the end result in order to keep our actions safe and ourselves intact" (p. 88). In these relationships with the schools' most precarious children – those who have experienced extreme trauma, are raising themselves, or are in care of the state – the teachers expose their own vulnerability: they risk themselves, they doubt their decisions, they are uncertain about the outcomes, and they experience and fear judgment from others. This, we believe, demonstrates the qualities of teachers' obligations to children; an unremitting commitment to an ethical response to the precarious Other while enduring the risks involved.

Teachers' Obligations to Precarious Others

Within the epistemological narratives of mastery, students are "framed" through discursive norms that operate "to produce certain subjects as 'recognizable' persons [making] others decidedly more difficult to recognize" (Butler, 2010, p. 6). In these stories, Brooke, Chris, and Jeanine, were indeed precarious – the ones who did not meet the prescribed norms. They were presumed to be known and knowable: dehumanized, objectified, and described as "slow," "lazy," "dull," "difficult," "likely to end up in jail," "worth good money," or simply, "bad." They were unrecognizable as "students" and as "children" and were at risk of being – and often were – conceived as lives unworthy of response. The educational system's frames are technologies of power that amplify the precarity of these already precarious children and are politically informed mechanisms to maintain the social order of things (Butler, 2004).

In the education system's epistemological endeavour that privileges knowledge, teachers are expected to be experts, to *know* and to propagate *knowing about* a child, enlisting hyperactive means of surveillance and assessment, identifying deficit and deviance, foreclosing differences, and ignoring the mysteries of the Other. It is this disposition of expert – the perseveration of knowing, recording, and classifying rather than being in an ethical relation with the Other – that can disturb the teacher. As we saw with Michelle and Faye, they were frustrated by the system that privileged rational knowledge (which manifested in testing and surveillance) over their understandings of teaching as being relationally oriented. However, these stories also illustrate teachers' strong sense of educational purpose and demonstrate "the very humility necessary for assuming responsibility" (Todd, 2003, p. 16) within technocratic education systems.

George's, Doug's, and Stacey's stories also illustrated the nuances of teachers' attempts to be in ethical relation with children: suspending judgments, maintaining an openness to their mysteries, waiting patiently, listening, and loving them. These teachers help us to see the qualities of teachers' obligation to children, centring unknowability and cultivating openness towards the Other – particularly with education's most precarious children. Although tasked with caring for so many children, these teachers engaged with those most precarious – those cast out by the system as unrecognizable. Their commitment to *learn from* the Other demonstrates their resistance to education's epistemological demands that arrive in advance, and their willingness to being changed by the encounter. Here, the teachers' sense of obligation is sparked by the precarity of the lives of the children whom they face, and we see in these teachers their attempts to apprehend the precarious Others beyond the frames of recognition. Thus, in cultivating ethical relationships – particularly with our most precarious children – teachers exhibit a tolerance for uncertainty, an openness to the differences of the Other, and a willingness to expose their own vulnerabilities. The ethical response is an unrelenting commitment – but also always a risk.

References

Ball, S.J. (2003). The teacher's soul and the terrors of performativity. *Journal of Education Policy, 18*(2), 215–28. https://doi.org/10.1080/0268093022000043065

Butler, J. (1997). *The psychic life of power: Theories in subjection*. Stanford University Press.

– (2004). *Precarious life: The powers of mourning and violence*. Verso.

– (2005). *Giving an account of oneself*. Fordham University Press.

– (2010). *Frames of war: When is life grievable?* Verso Books.

Cannella, G.S. (2000). The scientific discourse of education: Predetermining the lives of others – Foucault, education and children. *Contemporary Issues in Early Childhood, 1*(1), 36–44. https://doi.org/10.2304/ciec.2000.1.1.6

Caputo, J.D. (1993). *Against ethics: Contributions to a poetics of obligation with constant reference to deconstruction*. Indiana University Press.

Davies, B. (2006). Subjectification: The relevance of Butler's analysis for education. *British Journal of Sociology of Education, 27*(4), 425–38. https://doi.org/10.1080/01425690600802907

Janzen, M.D., & Phelan, A.M. (2018). "Tugging at our sleeves": Understanding experiences of obligation in teaching. *Teaching Education*, 1–15. https://doi.org/10.1080/10476210.2017.1420157

Janzen, M.D., & Schwartz, K. (2018). Behaving badly: Critiquing the discourses of "children" and their (mis) behaviours. *McGill Journal of Education/Revue des Sciences de l'Éducation de McGill, 53*(1), 109–27. https://doi.org/10.7202/1056285ar

Schinkel, A. (2017). The educational importance of deep wonder. *Journal of Philosophy of Education, 51*(2), 538–53. https://doi.org/10.1111/1467-9752.12233

Thomas, G., & Loxley, A. (2007). *Deconstructing special education and constructing inclusion* (2nd ed.). McGraw Hill.

Todd, S. (2003). *Learning from the other: Levinas, psychoanalysis, and ethical possibilities in education*. The State University of New York Press.

– (2004). Teaching with ignorance: Questions of social justice, empathy, and responsible community. *Interchange, 35*(3), 337–52. https://doi.org/10.1007/bf02698882

Chapter 2

Alienation and Exclusion: Appreciating Proximity

There have been lots of times when I've been overwhelmed.... Sometimes, trying to develop a community in the classroom felt impossible, and trying to meet so many needs, I felt like I was sinking. I remember driving home so many days just feeling like I was drowning because there was so much going on for those children. They were living hellish lives and I was trying to make their days at school happy.

– Lena, elementary school teacher

Canadian teachers are immersed in classrooms that are more diverse and complex than ever (Clandinin, Downey & Huber, 2009). This is evidenced by increased child poverty rates (Campaign 2000, 2015); increasing numbers of children in care of the state (Jones, Sinha, & Trocmé, 2015), with some provinces having the highest rates of children in care in the world (Brownell et al., 2015); increased racial, ethnic, and linguistic diversity (Statistics Canada, 2017); and the highest rates of inclusion of students with special needs in mainstream classrooms in the OECD countries (Evans, 2010). The diverse interests and needs of children place substantial demands on teachers who often experience children's requests, questions, anger, tears, confusion, and suffering as a form of incessant demand – not unlike someone "constantly tugging at [their] sleeves" (Caputo, 1993, p. 6).

Lena, a veteran teacher of thirty years, found her obligation to safeguard children and to advocate on their behalf overwhelming at times, so much so that she resorted to moving school districts, changing grade levels, isolating herself from other professionals, and finally, opting for early retirement. In so disengaging from the profession, she became an attrition statistic – another teacher who left the profession prematurely. At the nexus between obligation and disengagement, however, there is another story – that of a young child named James. Paradoxically, Lena had to distance herself from colleagues and other professionals in order to build a close relationship with James. In this chapter we explore the role of proximity, the necessity of disobedience, and the importance of imagination in ethical teaching. Lena's story helps to illustrate how obligation is an ordinary ailment of the teacher, a source of perennial anxiety and hope.

The Story of James

Lena enjoyed her work as a teacher, expressing her "joy of being with children every day" and that teaching had been "truly satisfying." It was apparent throughout Lena's descriptions of teaching that her work was guided by a deep sense of responsibility for children. She described her commitment to fostering a strong sense of classroom community while honouring each child's individual needs, interests, and hopes. Her descriptions of her deep commitment to particular children remained central in her interview and often illustrated the emotional toll of such commitment. One such boy, James, was described by Lena as the most non-compliant, violent, and challenging child she had ever encountered in her thirty-two-year career. Lena expressed feeling a tremendous sense of responsibility towards James, who had a difficult childhood, a complex familial situation, was extremely troubled, and had been deemed suicidal. James was seven years old.

Lena's sense of obligation to James rang through in our conversation with her, even though she had taught him several years prior to our interview. She conveyed the sense of urgency and desperation she felt at the time. Lena encountered James as a child in need of her help. As Caputo (1993) writes: "The power of obligation varies directly with the powerlessness of the one who calls for help, which is the power of powerlessness" (p. 5). Lena's feelings of obligation to James not only reflected James's desperate need for help, but also his proportionate inability to access it. James had few advocates: his father was absent and his mother, although very protective of him, struggled with issues related to complex poverty (Silver, 2016). Complex poverty extends beyond socio-economic deficiencies in income and includes "inadequate housing, low levels of education, poor health and self-esteem, relatively high exposure to violence," which "tends to be deep and long lasting and is often psychologically debilitating" (Silver, 2016, p. 94). James's mother was overwhelmed by the effects of her own family breakdown, unpredictable working hours often requiring that she work through the night, and by the extreme demands placed upon her by her son and his difficult and often violent behaviour. As a result, Lena felt responsible for James even when he was not at school, worrying about him constantly – as she drove home at night, and on weekends, always fretting about his well-being. Years later, we witnessed how Lena's experiences with James continued to haunt her as she persisted in working through her experiences with him.

Lena felt that James's mother, because of her own "difficult relationship with the school," was distrustful of school personnel, and so often "pushed any support away." Meanwhile, Lena actively sought more help for James, explaining, "I would send emails to the [school's support] team yelling, 'Help!' but [she pauses] there was no help." The team comprised other professionals, specifically a social worker and psychologist, both of whom never actually worked with James, in part because his behaviour was so difficult. The team had many meetings – some of which Lena was invited to – and provided periodic consultations. Lena was frustrated by the lack of support that was provided for James and felt abandoned and dismissed by the other professionals upon whom she called for help. Resigned to dealing with James alone, Lena explained that "we just kind of made it through every day as best we could [hoping] that I was able to make some difference in his life." Lena hoped that James knew that "there was somebody on his side." She remained his teacher for two years, feeling responsible, demoralized, and alone.

The Role of Proximity

The teacher's obligation – the unremitting requirement to respond to the vulnerable Other in each moment – is an affective enactment of the larger promise of an adult to a child. In Britzman's (2003) reading of Arendt, she states, "education is a promise" (p. 23), which helps us to conceptualize both the immediacy of the teacher's response (one's obligation) to the student and her commitment to the future. The promissory relationship between teacher and student involves a relentless demand to respond to the unforeseen needs of the Other and is a commitment to the student's immediate and future good. When conceived of as a promise between teacher and student, education is neither speculative nor hypothetical. The promise is performative, repetitive, and a commitment producing the event (Derrida, 2007). Yet, how does one respond to a student's uncontrollable sobbing or a physical outburst when the causes are complicated, the choices of response are numerous, and the outcomes of decisions are unknown? The teacher's obligation, therefore, is always fraught; it requires a response to something unforeseeable and which remains ultimately and always uncertain, unknowable, and likely inadequate.

Thus, as Derrida instructs, the promise is always also at risk; at risk of being threatened, betrayed, or perverted. Additionally, the promissory relation is "something beneficial and favourable" (Derrida, 2007, p. 458). Yet, because a teacher's response to a student is always uncertain, in that the impact of the teacher's response is always unknown in advance, the teacher's promise is always at risk of being broken. An explication of the qualities of this promissory relation, we believe, will help to illustrate the conditions necessary to foster ethical relationships within the current educational context.

Over the two years that Lena worked with James, she remembered the countless attempts she made to seek additional supports for him – yet, she recounted that neither the school psychologist nor social worker ever assessed James. In fact, James refused to cooperate with the other professionals when they would visit, observe, or talk with him. So eventually, they stopped trying. The professionals would, however, ask Lena questions about James and have "useless meetings" about him, recording their notes and adding them to James's growing file. After some time, the team of professionals compiled a report on James and provided it to Lena. Lena was outraged. She thought that their recommendations were "crazy" and were based on a child that "they had never even seen" and "only knew on paper." Lena was infuriated to read their "ridiculous" recommendations that, according to her, "were randomly pulled and cut-and-pasted into the report that they handed off to me." She felt undermined and that her concerns were not taken seriously, exclaiming as if speaking to the team of professionals, "What do you think I'm dealing with here?" She was infuriated by the lack of response to a child in such desperate need, exclaiming: "What are we doing? What are we doing for this child?" The other professionals' lack of understanding of James, of the extent of his violent behaviour, and of his tragic and incessantly demanding social and emotional needs were immensely frustrating for Lena. She simply could not understand their apparent lack of care for a child in such great distress. Ultimately, Lena balked at the report. She refused to implement what she characterized as "hair-brained" recommendations on account of her concern that they would damage the little progress she felt she had made with James, and so, she dismissed the experts and their report.

Lena perceived the team's recommendations as baseless: the team's physical and emotional distance from James meant that they could not understand him, she argued. Lena's assertions reflect the Levinasian idea that intimate proximity is required in order to encounter the vulnerability of the Other – "a space of the encounter with the other before calculation" or judgment (Edgoose, 2001, p. 126). Lena's sense of obligation to James was pressing and proximal; she was "face-to-face" with him in a way that the experts were not; their physical distance fostered their disassociation from James. In this sense, obligation exceeds rationality and reasonableness, and its affective urgency is neither transferrable to, nor acquired by, the experts via "the red flag emails" that Lena sent or the consultation meetings that took place. Lena's everyday physical and emotional proximity to James heightened her sense of responsibility to him but also exposed the risk of failing him and of breaking that fragile promise.

Growing increasingly desperate, Lena expressed deep frustration at the team's lack of knowledge about James and emphasized that James "wasn't heard" by them. Whereas the team of professionals attempted to learn about James through emails, meetings, and information provided by Lena, Lena's engagements with James were relational and attentive to his uniqueness. It was as if the team's attempts to learn about James amounted to little more than what Lena portrayed as the child "on paper," whereas her relationship with James was premised on "learning from the other," that is, a unique child in the context of a particular relationship (Todd 2003, p. 9). Educational relationships foster an attentiveness that recognizes differences, are openly receptive, and "resist codification" (p. 9) and preformed judgments. Lena's engagements with James were not based on technical responses informed by predefined rules or diagnoses of an objectified version of the child. For Lena, the ethical appropriateness of her response depended on the particularities – the uniqueness – of James. As Todd instructs, it is "the disruptive, unpredictable time of attentiveness to the Other where ethical possibility lies" (p. 9). The experts, relying on forms of knowledge of children and of practices that are finite, fixed and based on obtaining objective information about the Other, ultimately foreclose understandings of the uniqueness of each child.

In an attempt to uphold her promise to the child, Lena decidedly focused on patience and responsiveness to James. Feeling dismissed and demoralized by the other professionals, she acknowledged that she was left to work alone, knowing that she would have to "just figure it out and make it up as [she] went along." In addition to Lena's proximity and attentiveness, we see here another quality of the teacher's promise to the child, that of a commitment to a continuity of care. In other words, we see Lena's concern for James in the present and for the future. She worried about James in her daily contact with him, as well as when she was not at school, always wondering, "Is he safe?" Although committed to working with James, "trying to make it through each day," she expressed a deeper fear for his future, stating, "I don't think he'll make it to 18." Regardless of how fraught and elusive the teacher's commitment might be, Lena's promise is a promise of repetition – a commitment to each moment and to tomorrow (Derrida, 2007). And so, Lena continued to care for James, mostly alone. Although James was no longer at her school when we interviewed her – and it had been years since she taught him – Lena still worried about him: "I don't even know if he is alive, you know. He's the kind of kid, you know, he'll either be in jail or he'll kill himself." Lena faced the obligation to respond to James and his excessive violence, as well as his urgent need for compassion. She made judgments and then had to live with the unimagined consequences, all the while attempting to create the conditions for James to be recognized as a child in need of a response.

A Necessary Disobedience

Lena's refusal to enact the team's recommendations and her subsequent withdrawal from professional relations with team members constituted a necessary disobedience (Caputo, 1993). From Lena's perspective, disobedience was the only way she could uphold her promise to James. As Caputo (1993) reminds us, "it is precisely in the name of the Other, of justice, of respect, in the names of the children, that resistance is called for" (p. 119). Caputo insists that when "the sea of obligations in which we are immersed threatens to overwhelm us, to inundate and drown us … that is when we need resistance, not obedience" (p. 120). Thus, Lena's disobedience was necessary to uphold her promise to the child. She was indignant about the other professionals' treatment of James and their unconscionable recommendations based on an objectified child. Not only had they dismissed her requests for support based on her professional judgment of him, she had to witness the resultant institutional dehumanization of him. She refused to silently comply. Lena's necessary disobedience therefore became an ethical response, meaning that it was a response in which "there is no easy answer … no handy principle to which to appeal" – requiring that "we must respond to each individual and each situation anew according to its singularity" (Oliver, 2015, p. 489). Lena attempted to live out her ethical obligation, the impasse of the "impossible and unconditional" (Oliver, 2015, p. 489), in ways that the other experts did not.

A few days after the principal had denied yet another of Lena's requests for support for James, Lena found the principal "lurking in the hallway outside the classroom door" and "spying" on her and the children. She believed that the principal was trying to determine if she was "trumping up her observations" about James's behaviours. Again, she felt distrusted and her professional judgment undermined. By then,

Lena was already frustrated by the principal's "overly managerial" approaches, her "lack of understanding of early years" pedagogies, and her "anti-play" stance. With the budget for materials cut, the principal refused Lena's requests for funds for additional play materials, making her feel as though she had to "beg for money," and so Lena bought the play materials out of her own pocket. The principal's lack of pedagogical understanding, budgetary control, repeated requests that were not supported, and the surveillance of Lena reflect the ways in which principals' roles have become about regulation, foregrounding individual compliance and performance (Ball, 2003). These incidents added to Lena's growing sense of distrust of the other professionals, reinforced her feelings of isolation, and fuelled her active – and subversive – disobedience. In Lena's disobedience she resists what was expected of her by the principal, the professional others, and even the profession.

The year after James advanced to the next grade, Lena requested to be moved to kindergarten, an often-devalued sector of schooling, where she believed that "even [her] administrator didn't think it was all that important." Here, she hoped she would more easily be overlooked and left alone to do "good work with children," subversively teaching in ways that aligned with good practice and away from the undermining authority of the others, namely, the experts and her principal. Lena's increased distance between herself and the other professionals points to her symptoms of alienation. Lena described herself as a "lone wolf" and silently implored her colleagues to "ignore me all you want." Expressing a desire for detachment – "a paradoxical relation of relationlessness" (Clarke & Phelan, 2017, p. 21) – Lena actively sought to isolate herself rather than engage collegially and collaboratively with the school's social and professional context. Importantly, the "failures" or shortcomings of professional others – the social worker, psychologist, or principal – were not necessarily individual inadequacies, per se. Rather, their engagements – although inadequate in Lena's view – seemed to also be reflective of school district priorities and mandates. Regardless, Lena's move to kindergarten and her distancing from others became a subversive disobedience: an effort to maintain meaningfulness in her work while upholding her promise to children in a space where she hoped to be overlooked.

Yet, the sense of frustration with the demands of the system that ignored the complexities of children's lives eventually overwhelmed Lena. Bearing witness to the erosion of what she deemed as the educational purpose of schooling, Lena worried about the downward push of curriculum mandates and the principal's managerial practices of surveillance and budgetary austerity. She described feeling disconnected, demoralized, and frustrated, and stated that if the "system wasn't so broken," she might have stayed in teaching a little longer. Forced to witness an education system that she could no longer tolerate, Lena felt "powerless" and agonized about the state of education, saying, "I'm unsure what we're about anymore." Thus, after thirty-two years, Lena made a decision to retire early, stating: "If I was feeling really good about what we were doing, I might stay. But given the situation at my school, in my division, and in society in general, if I wasn't retiring early, I'd be looking for a different place." Lena resigned from the profession she loved because she could no longer tolerate what it had become and who it required her to be: a teacher whose obligations to the Other were overshadowed by expectations of curriculum mandates, other professionals' oversight of children they did not know, and an ongoing sense of surveillance and silencing.

Importantly, Lena's disengagement – enacted in her necessary disobedience in her refusal to comply with the other professionals' report, her self-alienation from her colleagues, and her eventual resignation – had negative implications not just for herself but for the profession. As Caputo (1993) argues, "exclusion and marginalization, thus, are never merely, formal ideas; they always have to do with damaged lives and disasters" (p. 119). The profession incurs a substantial loss: Lena's leadership and professional insight informed by her thirty-two years of experience and the ways in which this manifested in her pedagogical engagements with children. Her promise – a deep and ethical commitment to children – is paradoxically undermined by the institution she attempted to serve and subsequently prompted a loss for Lena, for children and their families, for her colleagues, and for the profession. Although Lena's disobedience was induced by her ethical obligation, it came at a cost, thus illustrating the experiences of obligation and the compounding emotional demands of teaching.

Imagination: Seeing Ethically

Expressing feelings of incompetence, powerlessness, and futility, Lena reflected:

> But I don't know. I don't know.... And it continued on. I mean I watched him go through our school and nothing ever really changed. Nothing ever really changed. He's not in our school anymore. I don't know. I really don't know what will happen to him. I really don't know.... We bear witness ... but are powerless in doing anything about it.

Lena's promissory relation, enlivened through her proximity to James's suffering, enacted by her attunement to his uniqueness, and expressed through the continuity of her commitment to him, constituted, in her own words, an attempt to "bear witness." In witnessing, Lena was not just an eyewitness of events, but rather was bearing witness, that is, she was attesting to James's suffering, to something beyond recognition and not necessarily seen (Oliver, 2015). She was compelled to bear witness to that which she did not know and to someone who was not recognizable: a young boy who would not be consoled or comforted by her usual pedagogical responses.

Bearing witness is a form of "ethical seeing," a "see[ing] from the heart" (Oliver, 2015, p. 482). It involves an affective transference of compassion, "something that pulls us outside of ourselves and toward another" (p. 482). Contrary to recognizing the Other according to preformed theories, assumptions, or beliefs, ethical seeing opens up a space of unrecognizability; appreciating the impossibility and unknowability of the other is precisely where ethics begins (Oliver, 2015). But it is also where uncertainty takes root. Lena described the way in which the thought of James kept her up at night: "I would think about what's happening to him on the weekends. Is he okay?" and, "What are we going to do for him?" In a state of Levinasian insomnia, Lena felt the weight of her responsibility to James, found herself dwelling on the child she did not really understand, and acknowledged the absence of simple solutions that might change his daily life and offer him a future (Oliver, 2015, p. 486).

Her own uncertainty and the inadequacy of expert responses threatened to undermine Lena's promise to James. However, one effect of the promissory relation – an unarticulated desire that things might be otherwise in the future, sanctioned by temporality and openness to the not yet – persisted. Caputo (2012) explains the promise as an event, "like a ghost whispering in our ear" (p. 27), making enticing commitments towards the future.

Because the future remains unforeseeable, a teacher's imagining of future possibilities for a child constitutes another form of ethical seeing. Eschewing a system that attempts to generalize children, erase their uniqueness, and dismiss their futures – via psychological profiling, testing, documentation of transgressions, diagnostic reports, and behavioural regimes – reflects Lena's imaginative capacity (Lear, 2006). Imagination requires commitment, courage, and hope in desperate times. Rather than rely on institutional practices that would have restricted creative thinking about the child, Lena recognizes her relationality with him, encountering him without subsuming his alterity (Todd, 2003). She tried to imagine James beyond his present circumstances – where he might be, what he might become, and how his life might be otherwise.

It is Lena's imaginative capacity that enables her to "respond better to the world's challenges" (p. 117) as they appear in her classroom in the person of James.

Lear (2006) argues that an imaginative capacity is a quality of a courageous soul, requiring that one encounters challenges in new ways, but also that in imagining the child's potentiality, there is a required appreciation of risk. It is as if Lena's deep sense of vulnerability in the face of risk (to herself, to the child, to the promise, and to the professional others) enables an openness and hospitality to the possible – however impossible it might be. Lear explains that "to be human is necessarily to be a vulnerable risk-taker; to be a courageous human is to be good at it. That is, a courageous person has the psychological resources to face the risks with dignity and to make good judgments in light of them" (p. 123). We see this courage in Lena's actions: in her commitment to children, in her rejection of the professional others, and in her disengagement from the profession which threatens her own recognizability. In Lena's courage, we see her "capacity for living well with the risks that inevitably attend human existence" (Lear, 2006, p. 121). Lena's capacity for risk is integral in her responsibility for the Other; in her obligation and promise to children. Yet, inexpressible in language, replete with gesture – tears, voice-breaking, stuttering, long silences – Lena bears witness to the tragic dimension of teaching, uttering, "I watched … every day; I hoped … I don't know." Never knowing for sure, fearing what she cannot know, changing her mind – and yet bringing an imaginative capacity to the child's future, beyond mere survival, amid the disappointment, failure, and disillusionment that has accompanied his life and his schooling experiences. Lena's imaginative capacity is an important quality of her promise to children, illustrating the strength of her obligation, even when the outcomes of the decisions are unknown. Her demonstrations of hope and imagination are what enliven her courage (Lear, 2006, p. 149), emphasizing that the good that might come about exceeds what can be conceptualized – it must be imagined.

Obligation as the Teacher's Ordinary Ailment

Lena's story conveys one teacher's experiences of obligation. In contemporary classrooms, where children like James arrive with significant needs, complicated by contexts of deficit and difficulty, we see the ways in which teachers, through their promissory relation to children, are called to bear witness. As an ethical responsibility, bearing witness requires decision-making in undecidable moments and creates a perpetual uncertainty (Oliver, 2015). As we see with Lena, this uncertainty resides not only in the moment, but the anxiety it evokes persists into the future. There is no escaping obligation; ethical responsiveness is both the teacher's greatest challenge and an ordinary ailment. Both Britzman (2003; 2006; 2009) and Oliver (2015) help us to see the links between the teacher's obligations and the dynamic relations between the self and the Other, in which the teacher is affected. As Butler (2004) reminds us, "Let's face it. We're undone by each other. And if we're not, we're missing something" (p. 23). In Lena's efforts to navigate the relational matrix and to uphold her promise to James, we witness the "intimacy of learning and the limits of what individuals can do for each other" (Berlant, 1997, p. 159). For Lena, it seems that bearing witness to the child became complicated by the expert others, resulted in her resistance, and became a way to attempt to maintain a fidelity to her promise to children. It is through her promissory relation to children, her active forms of resistance, and her imagined potential for children that we also see her courage in the commitment.

This conceptualization of teaching, occurring in the face-to-face encounters between teachers and students, shifts the emphasis of education from the fulfilment of mandates and implementations of outcomes, to that of recognizing the "the uncertainty and unpredictability of pedagogical encounter itself" (Todd, 2003, p. 28). It is in that uncertainty, in the obligation to the Other, that Lena exemplifies the courage required of teachers in order to respond ethically. We see in Lena's efforts that which "requires the ability to face up to reality, to exercise good judgment, and to tolerate danger in doing so" (Lear, 2006, p. 133). Lena's story illustrates the qualities of obligation and informs the emotionality entailed in teaching – specifically, understanding obligation not simply as a burden but as the ethical means through which teachers enact their promise to children. Lena helps us to understand the way in which obligation, interpreted through the promissory relation, becomes the impetus for teacher resistance, which provokes a reconsideration of teacher disengagement, not as a failure of the teacher, but as an effect of good teaching. In other words, while obligation requires the teacher to act on behalf of the child, at times it might also mean acting against the profession itself.

References

Ball, S.J. (2003). The teacher's soul and the terrors of performativity. *Journal of Education Policy, 18*(2), 215–28. https://doi.org/10.1080/0268093022000043065

Berlant, L. (1997). Feminism and the institutions of intimacy. In E.A. Kaplan & G. Levine (Eds.), *The politics of research* (pp. 143–61). Rutgers University Press.

Britzman, D.P. (2003). *After-education: Anna Freud, Melanie Klein, and psychoanalytic histories of learning*. The State University of New York Press.
– (2006). *Novel education: Psychoanalytic studies of learning and not learning*. Peter Lang.
– (2009). *The very thought of education: Psychoanalysis and the impossible profession*. The State University of New York Press.
Brownell, M., Chartier, M., Au, W., MacWilliam, L., Schultz, J., Guenette, W., & Valdivia, J. (June 2015). *The educational outcomes of children in care in Manitoba*. Winnipeg, MB: *Manitoba Centre for Health Policy*. http://mchp-appserv.cpe.umanitoba.ca/reference/CIC_report_web.pdf
Butler, J. (2004). *Precarious life: The powers of mourning and violence*. Verso.
Campaign 2000. (2015). *Let's do this – Let's end child poverty for good: 2015 report card on child and family poverty in Canada*. Family Service Toronto. http://campaign2000.ca/wp-content/uploads/2016/03/C2000-National-Report-Card-Nov2015.pdf
Caputo, J.D. (1993). *Against ethics: Contributions to a poetics of obligation with constant reference to deconstruction*. Indiana University Press.
– (2012). Teaching the event: Deconstruction, hauntology, and the scene of pedagogy. *Philosophy of Education Archive*, 23–34. https://educationjournal.web.illinois.edu/archive/index.php/pes/article/view/3597.pdf https://doi.org/10.47925/2012.023
Clandinin, D.J., Downey, C.A., & Huber, J. (2009). Attending to changing landscapes: Shaping the interwoven identities of teachers and teacher educators. *Asia-Pacific Journal of Teacher Education, 37*(2), 141–54. https://doi.org/10.1080/13598660902806316
Clarke, M., & Phelan, A.M. (2017). *Teacher education and the political: The power of negative thinking*. Routledge.
Derrida, J. (2007). A certain impossible possibility of saying the event. *Critical Inquiry, 33*(2), 441–61. https://doi.org/10.1086/511506
Edgoose, J. (2001). Just decide! Derrida and the ethical aporias of education. In G.J.J. Biesta & D. EgéaKuehne (Eds.), *Derrida and education* (pp. 119–33). Routledge.
Evans, P. (2010). Educating students with special needs: A comparison of inclusion practices in OECD countries. *Education Canada, 44*(1), 32–5. https://www.edcan.ca/wp-content/uploads/EdCan-2004-v44-n1-Evans.pdf
Jones, A., Sinha, V., & Trocmé, N. (2015). Children and youth in out-of-home care in the Canadian provinces. Canadian Child Welfare Research Portal (CCWRP) Information Sheet E, *167*, 1–4.
Lear, J. (2006). *Radical hope: Ethics in the face of cultural devastation*. Harvard University Press.
Oliver, K. (2015). Witnessing, recognition, and response ethics. *Philosophy and Rhetoric, 48*(4), 473–93. https://doi.org/10.5325/philrhet.48.4.0473

Silver, J. (2016). *Solving poverty: Innovative strategies from Winnipeg's inner city*. Fernwood.
Statistics Canada. (2017). Study: A look at immigration, ethnocultural diversity and languages in Canada up to 2026, 2011 to 2036. Government of Canada.
Todd, S. (2003). *Learning from the other: Levinas, psychoanalysis, and ethical possibilities in education*. The State University of New York Press.

Chapter 3

Shamed and Shaming: Honouring Students

It's like, um, the students that haunt me.... I'm not sure of the damage I did, or what I could have done to ... to try to remedy it.

– Tara, middle school teacher

Schools serve competing purposes, including socialization, qualification (or certification), and self-actualization (or subjectification) (Biesta, 2017; Egan, 2012). The role of summative assessment or evaluation – that is, the judgment of the merit, value, or amount of a student's learning – continues to be the primary mechanism in serving those purposes. The circulation of test scores, grades, report cards, and academic awards, for example, not only qualify students for future employment or further study, they also socialize students to accept competition as an essential, though punitive, part of the fabric of educational and social life. Importantly, student evaluation serves to convey the idea of a level playing field for all students if they apply themselves diligently to their schoolwork. There is little public acknowledgment that, "pupils are rewarded in examinations and assessed coursework for demonstrating precisely that knowledge which they are unlikely to have gained within the school" (Sullivan, 2001, p. 24). This is consistent with Bourdieu's (1977) claim that students from higher social classes are ensured educational success by virtue of the fact that it is linguistic ability and cultural knowledge – more strongly transmitted within the home than in school – that is examined and rewarded. The upshot is that some students thrive in schools and often leave with an inflated sense of competence (and entitlement), while others are left with a lingering sense of deflation, disappointment, and humiliation. While honour signifies academic success in the school context, shame clarifies just how much we care about what others think about us. When we fail in our attempts to impress others, we experience deep disappointment in ourselves to the point of shame.

Teachers like Tara are haunted by the thought of the damage done to students in the name of achievement and are uncertain about how to remedy the situation. A kind of fatalistic thinking takes hold whereby teachers, parents, and students believe that there is only a limited amount of something – academic success – available and that only those deserving receive their portion; there is a sense that that's all there is and that we are powerless to change it. Such belief is reinforced by practices such as the annual publication of school league tables based on standardized test results in some provincial newspapers (e.g., the *Vancouver Sun* in collaboration with the Fraser Institute, a conservative think-tank). In fatalistic systems, reputation is all and such publication makes or breaks school reputations, visiting honour or shame on associated communities, families, and teachers.

The retreat to fatalistic thinking seems inevitable in schools defined by the objects and processes of evaluation. In this chapter, we focus on the dynamic of shame in teaching, its politics (relations of power), and its ethics (openness to others) (Filiprovic, 2017). By focusing on one teacher's struggle with student evaluation, and her associated relations with parents, we wonder whether the ambiguity of shame as both (politically) problematic *and* (ethically) necessary might be resolved so that harm is minimized and difference maximized in schools (Caputo, 1993). Might ethics exceed politics in teaching even in these fatalistic times?

Fatalism: Honour and Shame

Fatalism was characteristic of pre-modern, honour-based societies (Visser, 2002). Fatalistic thinking insists on the idea that there is only a limited amount of something available; a sense that that's all there is. "Fate as portion is also a picture of the extent of ourselves: what we might call our capacities (the English term is itself a spatial metaphor) or our identity" (Visser, 2002, p. 37). The Greeks, Visser explains, preferred to speak of this as *timé* or honour, expressing not only fate but also as a relationship to others in society. Honour ascribed to us by other people dictates our portion or lot in life. "Honour arises from competition – it is always a matter of evident prowess – and is awarded by the people watching and deciding who has won" (Visser, 2002, p. 39). This means, of course, that one person's honour is increased at the expense of another's; there is a limited amount of honour to go around. As Visser explains: "Size is crucial – size that is relative to the 'extent,' or importance, of other people. Comparison is constantly made and competitiveness encouraged; negotiations are always ongoing, readjusting the importance allowed to each one by the others. Everybody is expected to try to be as 'big' as possible" (p. 37). Visser goes on to observe that, "There is something quasi-physical and therefore fated – an amount, a bodily factor, a percentage of a whole – about human worth. That we are what we do" (p. 41). Historically, honour related to who one was as judged by others, that is, a person's role or social definition (e.g., family name); some were perceived as wrong or shameful no matter what they did. A wronged person is reduced in size, as it were, and "must therefore seek revenge to retrieve the amount of honour lost" (p. 42). To be shamed is to be reduced in the eyes of others; it is about losing face or losing social standing. As such, shame announces the birth of the social and the ever-present possibility of losing others' approval.

Silvan Tomkins (1962/1992) captures Visser's understanding of shame as social loss in his conception of the affect polarity of shame-interest. Interest alludes to "a kind of affective investment we have in others," including human and non-human others (Probyn, 2005, p. 13). When that investment is thrown into question and "interest is interrupted, we feel deprived" because interest and enjoyment are linked (p. 13); and crucially, "that's when we feel shame" (p. 13). Shame underscores an intense attachment to the world, so when we "fail in our attempts to maintain those connections" (Probyn, 2005, p. 14), the experience of deep disappointment leads to a sense of shame.

Shame signifies the break in connection either between humans or between a person and an object. It is because we care about something or someone so much that we feel ashamed when that care is left unrecognized, not reciprocated, or insufficient. Because of the intensity of our desire to be connected, shame can be debilitating and prevent any further interest. The student's (or parent's) attachment to or interest in the test score as an object of achievement provides a sense of continuity about what makes their life meaningful and significant. For a student who desires but fails to achieve, be it a specific grade on a test or admission to an elite college, and the attachment that they long for is no longer possible, shame is felt "as an inner torment, a sickness of the soul" (Tomkins, fn. 27 in Probyn, 2005, p. 14).

Interestingly, however, shame is not a maudlin condition (Kosofsky Sedgwick & Frank, 2003). Unlike guilt, which is the result of some action (or inaction) one later regrets, shame is felt when one has done nothing wrong and yet, as a strong affect or undomesticated emotion, shame disturbs one's relation to oneself, other bodies, and histories. It is felt at different levels of intensity – shyness, embarrassment, humiliation – and "it produces effects – more shame, more interest – which may be felt at a physiological, social, or cultural level" (Probyn, 2005, p. 15). The power of shame is always incomplete, however; interest has been meddled with, obstructed even, but it has not been eliminated. As Probyn writes, "The body wants to continue being interested, but something happens to 'incompletely reduce' that interest" (p. 15). While we may continue "to spend time, money and labour" (Berlant, 2011) on the object – thereby endowing it with power and meaning – our interest is reduced because the loss is felt as at best threatening our well-being, or at worst "as a kind of living death" (Ahmed, 2014, p. 349).

There is a political saliency in understanding that affects, such as shame and interest, do things; they align individuals with communities – or bodily space with social space – through the very intensity of their attachment or interest. Nowhere is this more evident than in schools. This is because affects can move through the circulation of objects of achievement – test scores, achievement awards – as they flow between and among students, teachers, and parents. Such objects can become sticky, or "saturated with affect, as sites of personal and social tension" (Ahmed, 2014, p. 11) for all concerned. The upshot of the flow of affective objects is "the transformation of others into objects of feeling": the teacher becomes hateful for the parent, the student becomes frustrating for the teacher, and the revered teacher becomes an object of professional jealousy for colleagues. All are compelled to engage in and sustain the neoliberal fantasy of achievement via standardized tests, achievement scores and awards, rewards charts, and table points (Bibby, 2011).

The belief in fate and the associated logic of competition – to protect honour and avoid shame – takes on extreme proportions in neoliberal capitalism "with its either/or insistence on logically incompatible states of profit or loss, winners or losers, credit or debt, deserving or undeserving, [and] also dominates education through logics of pass or fail, effective or ineffective, above or below average" (Clarke & Phelan, 2018). Learning becomes a matter of constantly measuring up. The object of the test score, as an external good with its promise of the good life, now replaces the internal good of education as self-actualization, subjectification, or ethical self-formation in the late-Foucauldian sense (Ball & Olmedo, 2013). It is not that the promise of the test score is untrue but that in being true – in being "*too* possible" – that it becomes toxic (Berlant, 2011, p. 24; emphasis in original). What is cruel about these attachments and not just tragic, perhaps, is that: "The subjects who have x in their lives might not well endure the loss of their object/scene of desire, even though its presence threatens their well-being, because whatever the *content* of the attachment is, the continuity of its form provides something of the continuity of the subject's sense of what it means to keep on living on and to look forward to being in the world" (Berlant, 2011, p. 24).

The teacher's, student's, or parent's attachment to or interest in the test score as an object of achievement provides a sense of continuity about what makes their life/work meaningful and significant. Any threat to the achievement of the object – be it a specific grade on a test or admission to an elite college or apprenticeship program – can feel like a threat to life itself. So, cruel optimism is the condition of maintaining an attachment to or interest in a significantly problematic object despite, and in some sense because of, the threat that the attachment poses. This is because the very fear of losing the promising object, of relinquishing the quest to attain top scores and gain access to that sought after institution or career, "will defeat the capacity to have any hope about anything" (Berlant, 2011, p. 24). There may seem to be no other paths available for success: no other knowledge worthy of engagement other than that which leads to specified outcomes, no other image of self that can fulfil one's sense of the good, and no other work that can satisfy one's conception of the good life (Clarke & Phelan, 2015). Understandably, shame and hopelessness must be avoided at all costs. This is particularly true of middle-class parents whose anxious desire to hold on to advantages gained in the past thirty years is palpable (Smyth, 1992), and is often projected onto children and teachers.

Flirting with Fatalism

> It just is another feeling which has happened throughout the last decade of just feeling like the deck is stacked against doing what we know is … um, better. So that's super frustrating.
>
> – Tara, middle school teacher

Avoiding Humiliation: The Politics of Shame

Tara is a middle-school teacher who began her conversation with us by recalling an experience she had as a reluctant chair of her school's academic awards committee. She explained: "I just didn't really want to be part of the Student Achievement Awards committee, but it was one of those things which had been in place and nobody wanted to change it." Awards are objects signifying student achievement and as such they are a good example of how objects can become steeped in affect and sources of tension (Ahmed, 2014). Those who come into contact with them are transformed into objects of feeling. As committee chair,

Tara experienced public scorn when a disappointed parent who had expected her son to win the top academic award consistently spread rumours about her among the parent body. While Tara acknowledged "Daniel was gifted," she explained that "the award for academic excellence" required the student to have "straight A's and he didn't." As a result, "his parents were furious" and they attempted to retrieve their own and their son's honour through conversations with the vice-principal and subsequently with other parents. Honour is irretrievable in this instance and the shame lingers. Tara explained: "[F]ive years later, they're still mad and they're talking to people in the hallway, and I actually had to go up to them and say you know like three different times: 'Just come and talk to me!' I wasn't totally [sure] – I thought it was about the award but I didn't *really* know what it was about but I knew they had talked to the VP [Vice Principal] about it and they had talked to different parents and there was something that she [the mother] didn't want to even look me in the eye." Both teacher and parents felt humiliated and wronged. Shame is indicative of the "social bodying" of the subject (Foucault, 1977, p. 213) where "the panoptic eye of the public is the power gaze that shames in order to assimilate difference" (p. 213). Power announces itself in the burn of parental shame as the mother tries to account to other parents for her son not winning the award; or in the blushed cheek of the teacher as she passes the parent group in the hallway. What is the good of one's son being designated gifted if it is not publicly evident on awards night? What is the good of one's effort to be a good teacher when parents withdraw their respect? Moving beyond shame is difficult because of the power of the normative to hold sway and our desire to belong to the normative regime, to be a positive expression of it. As such, shame has an affective power that can be harnessed to inhibit and homogenize and to extort obedience and compliance. The goal is always to avoid shame: "Shame can work as a deterrent: in order to avoid shame, subjects must enter the 'contract' of the social bond, by seeking to approximate a social ideal. Shame can [then] also be experienced as *the affective cost of not following the scripts of normative existence*" (Ahmed, 2014, p. 107; emphasis in text). One could argue that all concerned – teacher, mother, and son – had entered the social contract that if one is highly competent and works hard, then one will be rewarded. The script of so-called normative existence – in which cultural and social practices such as awards night play a crucial part in distributing and legitimizing shame and honour – was to learn that one has little control ultimately. Achievement awards are at once inclusionary and exclusionary; there is always an affective dimension and it is through such affectivity that "the tyranny of power can rule democratically, that it can be articulated by the entire body of social relations" (Filipovic, 2017, p. 102).

Despite Tara's expressed misgivings about academic excellence awards in general and the competitive culture of her school in particular, she denied any wrongdoing as chair of the awards committee. Asserting that the committee had adhered to the rules throughout, she emphasized the fairness of procedures followed and asserted her innocence within a legalistic discourse. She is caught in a political trap that produces and maintains the teacher as central to a student's success as well as the one responsible for recognition of that success. As a result, she rationalized her humiliation by parents – "'Cause I didn't handle it well" – turning shame into guilt. Guilt paralyses can only be released via denial or confession, both involving "a subjection to the law" (Bryson, 2000, p. 367). Perhaps in such admission of complicity she believed that she could secure forgiveness and redemption.

In the event of the humiliated parent's second son entering her class, Tara approached the mother one more time: "[S]o I saw her in the hall and I was like you know we should really talk, like, she just like 'No, it's okay I'll stop talking about you. It's fine.'" There was no forgiveness or redemption for Tara. She had become at once the mediator of a family's shame and the target of their shaming. She felt complicit – for the power of her own gaze as it represented the normative panopticon of the school – but also resentful of feeling complicit. Nonetheless, while she knew the game that was afoot – its cruel optimism (Berlant, 2011), as it were – she could not admit to the problematics of awards or academic competition to the parents without sacrificing the integrity of her colleagues, her school, and the teaching profession. "I'd like people to see teachers as committed in like, um, not harried and just surviving but actually committed to, um, to teaching … there's excellent things going on. Right? … for people to see that excellence…. So, I think that, um, it creates a kind of, um, insecurity or concern that, um, that, uh, the ideas around teachers as not being hard working, not being academic or, um … not being caring?" The intensity of affect associated with a single parent seeped through all parent relations and steered Tara towards fatalistic thinking: "Chances are that you won't be successful whatever you do; it's not easy to be successful as a teacher." Feeling scapegoated, stigmatized, and shamed (by parents) over several years, she shared: "[t]here's a couple of them that hate me. I'm sure of it." She felt excluded from those conversations "that happen on the playground … or outside the classroom." Put simply, Tara felt deprived of the very relationships in which she was most interested. Shame had clarified previously unknown or underappreciated investments. She admitted: "[W]hatever sense of obligation I have to the kids it's lighter than the sense that I have to the parents." Conflict with parents constituted exposure and failure: "[T]hey don't have confidence in me being the teacher or they're angry with me because they don't like what I've said." She continued, "A negative conflict" with "just one parent" in a given year is to be avoided at all costs, she explained, because "it dominates ... [and] can occupy so much headspace."

Tara experienced the discomforting and perplexing self-conscious awareness that another's gaze can induce; it revealed only inadequacy when compared to her best sense of herself as a teacher or those teachers by whom she measured herself (Tarnopolsky, 2004). Her depiction of the relationship with one parent conveys an assemblage of energies, words, gestures, commitments, and bodily feelings (Mulcahy, 2012). The vengeful parental body provoked strong affects as the usual "veil of civility" that routinely conceals animus between parents and teachers from plain sight is lifted (Elsthain, endnote 13 in Tarnopolsky, 2004).

In its politics, shame is manifested as "an intensification of power" that includes by exclusion (Filiprovic, 2017, p. 102). The foregoing narrative underscores the way in which all students are included in the competition of awards by virtue of their ultimate exclusion from the prize. The power relations between parent and teacher are magnified and dramatized as "egoisms struggling with one another ... in the commerce of rights and concessions" (Levinas in Filiprovic, 2017, p. 109) – a teacher unable to relinquish her role in a system committed to competition pitted against a parent unwilling to forego the honour bestowed by an academic award. Shame circulates: is the best one can do is to try to avoid it?

Avoiding Wrongdoing: An Ethics of Shame

While politics emphasizes the avoidance of shame, ethics recommends the avoidance of wrongdoing itself. In fatalistic institutions such as schools, the avoidance of wrongdoing proves challenging for teachers. Many of the teachers in our study expressed deep concern about the dominant and often destructive role of evaluation.

The partiality of evaluation – its incomplete and necessarily biased dimensions – bothered Tara a good deal. She described student evaluation as an experience of "always wondering and wandering about in the dark, catching glimpses which may not accurately represent [student] experience; what we catch may be a fleeting moment for the child." It was the "students who haunted [her]," she explained in reference to the effects of student evaluation and "the damage [she] did, or what [she] could have done to try to remedy it." This was the case particularly during reporting periods when she was compelled by the school system to sum up a student's learning in terms of "a list of learning outcomes with check marks … and a sheet of letter grades." Speaking of report cards, Tara exclaimed: "I hate them! I hate them!" She described how she witnessed the shame of students who felt they were "stupid" while she characterized parents as "worship[ping] at the altar of the report card." Tara's appreciation of student vulnerability served to remind her of her own complicity in grading and reporting student performance; she felt ashamed of her perceived cruelty to those students who were already vulnerable in a competitive school culture. Here shame is an ethical index of the teacher's constitutive openness to her students: "Shame can only emerge in sincerity of an ethical relation where the frailty of the other reflects my own inhumanity" (Filipovic, 2017, p. 109).

The students' frailty and the teacher's shame reveal the weight of the normative order of schooling – surveillance, judgment, and reporting – as well as the community's desire to reaffirm its values – achievement, competition, and hierarchical order. However, Tara's concerns signal the potential collapse of the teaching subject who is no longer able to support that order. The teacher is unable to hide herself from others, but her concerns reveal her as a "willing captive of others" (Filipovic, 2017, p. 109). Shame confronted her with herself; she was ashamed of what she was required to do within the system, but she could not escape; she had to assume the very impossibility of being herself. Shame courses a passage between subjectification and de-subjectification. Finally stripped of subject positions, the subject confronts and resists its vulnerability. It is here, however, that ethical relations become possible. In experiencing shame, Tara experienced "Levinas's ethical consciousness divested of interest [her reputation as a teacher of so-called high-achieving students] and traumatized to the marrow by a failure of responsibility" (p. 110).

Within a politics of shame, the effort was focused on adults' (teachers' and parents') avoidance of humiliation. Within an ethics of shame, the emphasis is on avoiding wrongdoing in the first instance. Tara was committed to "trying to convince the parents to see their child differently," but she also understood that any effort to do so had to abide by the institutional requirement to evaluate and report student learning within recognizable and official forms. So, her efforts to avoid wrongdoing – the shaming of students – took the form of dilution and distraction.

In an attempt to dilute or manage families' anticipated affective reactions to the report cards, Tara organized in-person meetings between each student and their parents: "If I have the meetings leading up to it there won't be as strong a reaction to the report card and it won't be shocking or you know there'll be less conflict? But I don't know if that's true." The desire to avoid or contain conflict with parents suggests how public and debilitating such conflict can be. She was fearful of the consequences that might ensue, particularly for students when parents confront the "shocking" low achievement of their children. When students expressed fear of questioning and challenging teachers and parents – who Tara characterized as "scary adults" – she invited students to complete their own report card first – a self-evaluation – with the view of informing the teacher's final report card. Instead of dissipating the impact of the report card, however, self-evaluation became saturated with other affects for some students. "There are always kids who don't want to do that. Because I think it terrifies them to tell me something other than what they think I want to hear. And so, um, I've been trying to break that down where, um, when they just like throughout the year do the one-on-one around different little tests and I tell them, you know what, you need to *practise* talking to scary adults about things that, um, you want to challenge." Framing self-evaluation as a courageous counternarrative to that of the teacher's evaluation was juxtaposed to the discomfort of sitting one-on-one with the teacher – in confessional mode. Was the student anticipation of being shamed by the forthcoming report card heightened? Tara acknowledged: "my perception of how heavy it is ... really coming from the faces I notice in the room." The students are surfaced as the injured party, the ones hurt by evaluation policies and practices.

Again, in an attempt to avoid wrongdoing, minimize harm, and manage affects associated with evaluation and reporting, Tara opted for a strategy of distraction. She distributed each final report card in what she called "a loot bag": "And I try to make the report cards come in an envelope and I try to make it a loot bag, so I'll put in candies and I'll put in poems. I'll try to write them a little note. So, I try to have many things in there. And then hoping those things occupy more of their focus than the.... (she trailed off)." By producing distractions, the hateful object – the report card – was reframed as something fun or enjoyable; the interest in achievement and the anticipation of shame were replaced momentarily by an interest in a pleasurable distraction. At least that was the teacher's desire.

Shame aligns teacher and student as objects of parental criticism but also as victims of a system whose very social utility is to spur achievement in children. Shaming is "heavily directed at children as part of their socialization" (Stearns, 2017, p. 77). Some students, as Tara explained, "hide their schoolwork" from the teacher and have their parents do their homework because they feel "overwhelmed with what [is] going on in the class." The circulation of report cards, however, can also realign parents and students as parents "blame [particular teachers] for the student not doing as well as he once did." Children's shame over adult evaluation of their performance surfaces the failing teacher even as it exposes the failing student. The exposure of failure is crucial to fatalism. Students are required to remain in school, but teachers can leave – and they do. Tara hinted at that very possibility: "There's only so many times that I think you can feel like you're not doing the job you want to do before you want a different job. Especially if you feel like it's out of your control."

Beyond Fate: Can Ethics Exceed Politics in Teaching?

As we witness the dynamic of shame in Tara's textured narrative, we sense a mode of living as a teacher as it comes into being – the hopes, the promises, the disorientations, the intensities, and few, if any, resting places. Bodies are on alert – marked, readily engaged, always talking, "exercising a capacity to affect and to be affected" (Stewart, 2010, p. 343). What is surfaced in Tara's story is obligation as "a form of attending to what is happening, sensing out, accreting attachments and detachments, differences and indifferences, losses and proliferating possibilities" (p. 343). For this teacher, encounters with parents and their children, school objects, and events (in classrooms, hallways, or playgrounds) lay tracks of interest, recognition, resentment, prejudice, fear, shock, relief, anticipation, attunement, and shame. As a result, there is a lingering feeling of powerlessness and fatalism, reminding us of Caputo's (1993) ethics.

Caputo's (1993) ethics can be summed up in the spirit of minimizing harm and maximizing difference. To minimize harm to others is, for Caputo, to recognize and bear witness to others' vulnerability as sufferers of indignity via humiliation or cruelty. By maximizing difference, he is against "any defining and confining determination of human being that tries to impose limits on the diversity of what we can be and on what is coming" (p. 15). Rather than build fences to contain the possibilities of the young, he might argue that we maximize different understandings of what it means to be good. Evil, he says, is always the same: it always causes needless suffering. To be ethical in our dealings with one another, in Caputo's sense of the term, therefore, is to be *for* novelty. To be ethical is to be educational, we would argue; both are about inviting the newness – a singular capacity for originality, creativity, and dissent – each young person introduces to the world.

Schools have rarely been about novelty but have always been about normalization. Achievement trumps all other educational goals and undergirds schooling as its singular, standardized interest. Pervading everyday practices and encounters, achievement is *the* vehicle for student shame, parental embarrassment, teacher (in)dignity, and school pride (or shame). Objects of achievement – awards, diplomas, tests, report cards – are ubiquitous, giving shape and being shaped by the affects that saturate them and those bodies with whom they come into contact. The everyday affects of achievement are difficult, some would say impossible, to escape in school. Unless perhaps one can create a form of life that exists alongside the institution of schooling, but which does not succumb to it. Some teachers may create such a life, managing to live and teach alongside the mainstream institution carving out spaces for the recognition of marginalized others. To feel a little less entangling or fatalistic, ethical obligation may have to be lived in parallel where there is space to bear witness to others as sufferers of indignity, humiliation, or cruelty. Tara bore witness to students' vulnerability in an institution we might characterize as "haughty and proud, deeply filled with shame," endowed with private interest rather than public purpose (Probyn, 2010, p. 82). That said, in an effort to reimagine less restrictive and less fatalistic forms of educational life, Tara's loot bags – though meagre efforts to minimize shame via dilution and distraction, yet overshadowed by the system's demand for display of achievement – were perhaps examples of generative repetitions of care and possibility that enable her and her students to hold on to the world for now.

While some may believe Tara's efforts paltry at best, we might remember teaching through "the transmission of affect" and the uncertain force of its promise in schools is neither straightforward nor easy (Stewart, 2010, p. 353). This teaching is, however, "life itself" (p. 353).

References

Ahmed, S. (2014). *The cultural politics of emotion*. Edinburgh University Press.

Ball, S. J., & Olmedo, A. (2013). Care of the self, resistance and subjectivity under neoliberal governmentalities. *Critical Studies in Education, 54*(1), 85–96. https://doi.org/10.1080/17508487.2013.740678

Berlant, L. (2011). *Cruel optimism*. Duke University Press.

Bibby, T. (2011). *Education – An 'impossible' profession? Psychoanalytical explorations of learning and classrooms*. Routledge.

Biesta, G. (2017). *The Rediscovery of teaching*. Routledge.

Bourdieu, P. (1977). Cultural reproduction and social reproduction. In J. Karabel & A.H. Halsey (Eds.), *Power and ideology in education*. Oxford University Press.

Bryson, M. (2000). Guilt and education. *Philosophy of Education Annual Yearbook*, 365–8.

Caputo, J.D. (1993). *Against ethics: Contributions to a poetics of obligation with constant reference to deconstruction*. Indiana University Press.

Clarke, M., & Phelan, A.M. (March 2015). Negativity, cruel optimism and the virtue of impotentiality in education. Presented at the Philosophy of Education Conference, Oxford University, England.

– (2018). Beyond reproductive futurism and cruel optimism: Teaching–learning as world spectatorship. [Unpublished Manuscript].

Egan, K. (2012). Competing voices for the curriculum. In S.E. Gibson (Ed.), *Canadian curriculum studies: Trends, issues, and influences* (pp. 45–62). Pacific Educational Press.

Filipovic, Z. (2017). Towards an ethics of shame. *Angelaki, 22*(4), 99–114. https://doi.org/10.1080/0969725x.2017.1406050

Foucault, M. (1977). *Discipline and punish*. Pantheon.

Kosofsky Sedgwick, E., & Frank, A. (2003). *Touching feeling: Affect, pedagogy, performativity*. Duke University Press.

Mulcahy, D. (2012). Affective assemblages: Body matters in the pedagogic practices of contemporary school classrooms. *Pedagogy, Culture & Society, 20*(1), 9–27. https://doi.org/10.1080/14681366.2012.649413

Probyn, E. (2005). *Blush: Faces of shame*. University of Minnesota Press.

– (2010). Writing shame. In M. Gregg and G.J. Seigworth (Eds.), *The affect theory reader* (pp. 71–90). Duke University Press.

Smyth, J. (1992). Teachers' work and the politics of reflection. *American Educational Research Journal, 29*(2), 267–300. https://doi.org/10.3102/00028312029002268

Stearns, P.N. (2017). *Shame: A brief history*. University of Illinois Press.

Stewart, K. (2010). Afterword: Worlding refrains. In M. Gregg and G.J. Seigworth (Eds.), *The affect theory reader* (pp. 339–53). Duke University Press.

Sullivan, A. (2001). Cultural capital and educational attainment. *Sociology 35*(4), 893–912. https://doi.org/10.1017/s0038038501008938

Tarnopolsky, C. (2004). Prudes, perverts, and tyrants: Plato and the contemporary politics of shame. *Political Theory 32*(4), 468–94. https://doi.org/10.1177/0090591704265523

Tomkins, S. (1992). *Affect, imagery, consciousness*. Springer. (Original work published 1962)

Visser, M. (2002). *Beyond fate*. Anansi Press.

Chapter 4

Destitute and Dying: Preserving Dignity

This girl [Linh] ... was covering herself over with a freeze blanket, standing over a garbage can, eating out of a can, and just sobbing.

– Shihmei, high school teacher

Tears streaming down her face, Shihmei describes her encounter with Linh, an international, homestay student at her secondary school, a victim of physical and emotional neglect. In this chapter we describe similar encounters between teachers and students and explore teachers' experiences and understandings of their obligation to preserve the inherent dignity of students, to guard against exploitation, and to alleviate suffering (van Manen, 2012). In the face of death and deprivation, we consider the obligation to care as a form of madness, exceeding the boundaries of the rational economy of care that often characterizes teaching.

An Economy of Care

In loco parentis is a legal principle that binds teachers to the role of *careful parent* in relation to their students. Care, by this official accounting, is a form of "serious speech" that regulates the common discourse of the profession as "a rational community" (Lingis, 1994, p. 112). Seriousness is "the weight of the rational imperative that determines what is to be said" (Lingis, 1994, p. 112). The teaching profession, including teachers, school leaders, and educational researchers, conceives of teachers' care of students as something fundamentally desirable, with some asserting that there is no education without a relation of care (Bingham & Sidorkin, 2004; Noddings, 1984; van Manen, 1994). In this view, "relation [encounter and response]" is conceived as "ontologically basic and the caring relation [as] morally basic" such that we "become individuals only within relations" (Noddings, 1984, p. 101). The carer is characterized as one who is engrossed (in a state of concern or worry about someone or something), committed (exemplifying continuity of care), and attentive (prioritizing the projects of the cared-for over one's own) (Noddings, 2012).

Noddings's (1984) discussion of natural caring is of particular interest here. Noddings refers to moments when our inclination to care for others "naturally arises, as a feeling, an inner voice saying, "I must do something" (p. 81). In such moments we are not moved by ethical codes and "there is no demand to care" (p. 81). Noddings (1984) explains: "We cannot demand that one have this impulse ['I must'], but we shrink from one who never has it. One who never feels the pain of another, who never confesses the internal 'I must' that is so familiar to most of us, is beyond our normal pattern of understanding. Her case is pathological, and we avoid her" (p. 81).

In the context of teaching, however, Jung (2015) wonders, "how we prevent 'I must' from quickly becoming an excessive inclination" (p. 62). Valuing rectitude, Jung's concern is to avoid inclining too much towards the Other lest one finds oneself battling bad feelings: those feelings that result from the sense of not doing enough, not doing it well enough, and not being better at it (Janzen & Phelan, 2020; Ruti, 2018). Connell (2009) argues that teachers have to manage the flow of their own (and their students') emotions if good teaching is to be sustainable. Feelings can be tempered by logic and reason, of course. Teachers are capable of analysing the situation at hand, of assessing the needs of others, and of evaluating whether the necessary human or material resources are available to them. As a result, some may choose to ignore the impulse of "I must" while others will make an alternative judgment. Thought about in this way, the role of the teacher as careful parent is a matter of practical wisdom or *phronesis*, where a reasonable balance is sought between care for the self and care for others.

Caputo (1993) leans towards Noddings's conception of natural caring. He is keen to differentiate phronetic care, the result of practical wisdom (*phronesis*), from obligation. He views *phronesis* as of the order of *nous*, a matter of practical intelligence – primarily cognitive, rational, and "not exactly of having a heart" (p. 117). While phronesis is concerned with the subtle idiosyncrasies of "a complicated and slightly unprecedented situation" (p. 117), it is, for Caputo, "the virtue of the hale and the whole, of the best, with those who deserve honour" (p. 117). By contrast, the *argumentum ad misericordiam*, or appeal to pity, "is directed at the worse, who excel at nothing" (p. 117). He writes: "The *argumentum ad misericordiam* is not a matter of practical intelligence but of a certain succumbing to the claims of the Other, a giving in, a melting, a surrender, a loss of self; not *nous* but *kardia*.... But the *argumentum ad misericordiam* [appeal to pity] answers the claims that disasters put upon us, which looks a little mad; and its opposites are the ones who are smart enough to take care of themselves, those who know who is number one, who prefer to go first class *(glas)*" (Caputo, 1993, p. 117).

While it seems to us that *phronesis* is what is called for in schools most of the time, there are situations where logic and reason have a limited, if any, role to play in caring – when one is taken over or overtaken by unexpected events. In such cases, "excessive inclination" (Jung, 2015, p. 62) might be precisely what is called for – where the teacher is confronted by the "one who has been laid low, to victims and outcasts" and where one's obligation is to reduce and alleviate suffering, not to produce it, not to augment it" (Caputo 1993, p. 145). Obligation to those who have not gotten as far as freedom and autonomy – students like Linh, perhaps – may require more than reasonable care, more than what the usual economy of care dictates for teaching. What might it mean, for example, for teachers to reach out to those who are deprived, who are "muted, silent, even invisible" (p. 115), and to give them a lift and provide some relief?

Those teachers who succumb to appeals to pity may appear mad and foolish in Caputo's (1993) terms. The essence of good sense for the teacher, perhaps, is to avoid obligation and not to be "moved," "touched," "melted," or "softened" (p. 218). The professional impulse may be to avoid inclining too much towards the Other; enough care but not too much is warranted – this is the reasoned and reasonable characteristic of *phronesis*. Caught in a model of teacher–student relationship that is "already installed and institutionalised for the economical provision of care" (Verwoert, 2009, p. 166), some teachers may be at best characterized by colleagues as caring too much, a little over the top or off-kilter, or at worst as being manipulated by students and in need of guidance. A kind of measured moralism sets in.

In the research literature, excessive inclination is viewed as the precursor of teacher burnout. The term burnout refers to "a process in which an individual's natural resources (i.e., stress responses, coping abilities, resiliency, etc.) are being used in excess due to their occupational demands.... Although emotional exhaustion is the defining feature of burnout, depersonalization and loss of feelings of personal accomplishment characterize this experience" (Marko, 2015, p. 2). These discourses of teachers' mental health materialize in the measurement of teachers' psychological well-being through such means as the K–6 Mental Health

Screening Tool, the Teacher Burnout Inventory, the World Health Organization Quality of Life Scale, Attitudes Towards Seeking Professional Psychological Help-Short Form, Social Stigma Scale for Receiving Psychological Help, and the Trait Emotional Intelligence Questionnaire – Short Form. It seems that for teachers to meet the occupational demand to care, they must exhibit balance (i.e., balanced lifestyle, not to care so much that it hurts), self-care, and emotional intelligence; maintaining balance requires an appropriate distance from students.

However, we would like to think about the obligation to care outside of an economy of care and its concomitant moralism and consider why it might be advisable to do so. "Could there be a way of giving, receiving, and calling for care that goes beyond such economic contracts [or systems of care]" (Verwoert, 2009, p. 166)? This question is important because it can alert us to the complicated ways in which care circulates in schools, as well as enables us to challenge assumptions about the teaching profession.

We have chosen to examine the *eccentricities* of care by focusing on limit situations in which teachers find themselves recognizing an imperative to care that goes *beyond* its rational or institutional form. Limit situations are experiences when we face death, pain, suffering, and failure and in doing so are confronted with ourselves in often profound ways. Shihmei speaks of her encounter with Linh, a deprived and anxious student. Justin tells the story of a death on the playground of his school – on one of his first days teaching in the so-called worst performing secondary schools. Ian tells stories of threatened school closure in a low-income, immigrant neighbourhood where the high dropout rate is a well-kept secret. Doug is a school counsellor who tells the story of Stephen's suicide attempt and subsequent homelessness. Teachers' stories are tragic; they describe student distress, suffering, and destruction; and they spell disaster and impossibility. In limit situations, teachers are moved to respond but find themselves at the limit of "serious speech" (Lingis, 1994, p. 112): their colleagues do not share their language nor do they understand their concerns or actions. They become troubled; their everyday teaching lives interrupted; their relation to themselves, other bodies, and histories disturbed; and they experience their own frailty, susceptibility, and mortality.

Teachers' accounts of stirring encounters with students suggest four gestures of eccentric care: being moved and caught off guard, taking a leap of faith, becoming politically conscious, and, finally, creating intimacy. The typical contract between the teacher and student that would otherwise govern care is interrupted and what is exposed is the potentiality of teachers and students "living together in a space ungoverned by any economy" (Verwoert, 2009, p. 172). This is not to say, however, that each gesture is devoid of a relation of power.

Eccentricities of Care

Being Moved and Caught Off Guard

Shihmei cries as she describes her encounter with Linh, an international, homestay student, in the schoolyard. Linh is standing over a garbage bin, wrapped in a freeze blanket, eating food from a can and sobbing. Shihmei describes the moment: "I taught her for years and had no idea why she looked so tired. So tired, having a lot of difficulty keeping up with her studies ... living in these horrible living conditions, still having to work, and still having to pretend that she's happy to her parents. Her parents are working hard [in her home country] ... making a small amount of money and all she can think about is, 'How can I, how can I do something for my parents?'" Shihmei is moved by Linh's bodily exhaustion, hunger, and distress – all of which attest to physical and emotional neglect and how exploitative child labour, in the name of international educational opportunity, threatens inherent human dignity. "International students don't fall under one definition," Shihmei explains, "some come from abroad with a bare minimum of money to live on" and have to "work illegally in restaurants, house cleaning, and nail salons." Linh, she recalls, was working part-time for her uncle in his restaurant; and, because she was living in his basement for free, "she was paid minimum [wage], expected to do all the house chores, cooking, cleaning, and grocery shopping."

Here we witness how the obligation to care happens "wherever the power of powerlessness surges up and touches us, for flesh does not have an identifiable gender, a proper family name, a national identity" (Caputo, 1993, p. 173). Care is a different kind of power – it comes from the outside, from the powerless; "it is a feeling that grows in strength directly in proportion to the desperateness of the situation of the other" (Caputo, 1993, p. 5). The power to care comes from someone else – a response to a call from elsewhere. There is no time for doubt, no zone of neutrality or impartiality – the teacher immediately feels the student's pain and sorrow. She is caught off guard by "the image of sensual suffering" (Lingis, 1994, p 15).

Care, therefore, is a different kind of power because it is a call that comes from the outside, from the powerless (Lingis, 1994). Care is not a manifestation of one's own power to do this or that, but "is something that one is empowered to do by someone else to whose needs one responds" (Verwoert, 2009, p. 165). "Once that need is acknowledged there is no way back; you receive the power to care. This power does not have as its source … some talent or potential rooted in the self, an ability to perform that you would have because you are so potent or brave, but is something that arrives to you from the outside" (Verwoert, 2009, p. 166). In considering Shihmei's account about her student Linh, we are struck by the manner in which the "I" of the teacher inclines in the face of the student's distress; the teacher is unable "to control that inclination" (Lingis, 1994, p. 18). Shihmei's tears suggest that she is reduced to a kind of suffering that comes when thought is no longer in command. The teacher is afflicted with the imperative that issues from a particular student's suffering. Pulled up short, the I's intentions contested, the teacher falters and hesitates, both animated and wearied by the appeal of the Other. She is at once moved and overwhelmed as the ethical complexities of international study (Stein, de Oliveira Andreotti, & Suša, 2019) are laid bare. Here we witness the ill-considered impact of international education, which originally, perhaps, held an educational and cultural focus, and has since become an economic endeavour (Elnagar & Young, 2021).

Being touched by the student's plight, the teacher is reconfigured from an autonomous agent into a heteronomous one (Caputo, 1993); the teacher is exposed. Caputo explains, "being touched is the vulnerability, susceptibility, or sensitivity of the I to the power that emanates from the Other" (p. 217). The teacher feels the pain of the other and this is the vulnerability of the agentic body of the teacher, of her free and autonomous self-possession in the face of the "sensuous singularity" (Lingis, 1994, p. 18) of the suffering student.

While she feels the impulse to care – the "I must" – she is overwhelmed by Linh's situation and its entanglement in political, economic, educational, and familial discourses. Feeling "horrified … beyond belief," Shihmei worries that she "cannot do much." Yet her sense of vulnerability and limitation mobilizes her to action. Her immediate response is to ensure that the student is fed and clothed appropriately for the Canadian winter, but ultimately, the event moves her to leave full-time teaching, begin graduate studies, and engage in a form of activist scholarship, devoting her graduate research to the plight of international students in Canada.

Taking a Leap of Faith

I'm not waiting…. I'm just saying okay I'll just start taking that leap of faith and just saying let's just see what happens, like go ahead and start acting as if….

(Justin, high school teacher)

As a newcomer to an Indigenous community in the rural interior, Justin is surprised by teaching colleagues who make no effort to participate in the local community, by the absence of resources with which to implement a drama program, and by the complete lack of extracurricular activities for youth. Recognizing the systemic, institutional failure at play in the school and its community, he is "haunted by what insists in the midst of what exists" (Caputo, 2012, p. 32). He witnesses history in the "cracks and crevices" of the present; it is a history of cultural genocide and obligation that haunts him. During our interview with him, Justin pauses as if to address his Indigenous students directly: "How do I, how do I achieve that? I can't. I can't fix so much that ... that you need fixed.... There's only so much that I *can* do and from a thirteen-year-old's or five-year-old's perspective, is that enough?" Not unlike Shihmei, Justin is acutely aware of his limits as a teacher. Borne of his own biography – his self-declared search for community as a gay man – he appears open to the possibility of reimagining ways of relating with students, colleagues, and community members. As if in response to his own questions, he recalls an encounter with one of the community elders who asks that Justin respect the students and have high expectations for them. Justin worries about making promises he cannot deliver. The risk is palpable. Then something happens.

In the aftermath of the accidental death of an Indigenous student on the school playground, Justin attends several ceremonies hosted by the student's community. He describes a moment during one of the ceremonies: "One older student in the class ... touched my shoulder .... And that was really powerful and made a big difference in the support that I felt." Contact and accompaniment are important when language does not have the power to say what has to be said because sometimes words appear "vacuous and absurd" (Lingis, 1994, p. 108) or because institutional hierarchy forbids it. Justin interprets the student's gesture as a sign of care. His perception of how he fit within the community changed. He felt supported, cared for, and encouraged, not by his colleagues or the school system, but by the Indigenous community.

Justin's experience of care from the Indigenous student becomes pivotal. Believing in what might be possible in the midst of the impossible is an act of faith. Despite the historical precarity of the school community, the insecurity of his own teaching position, Justin makes what he characterizes as "a serious commitment" to the student council to raise $22,000 to collaborate with them to create a school drama program. Could he/they accomplish the task? Could he/they raise the necessary funds? Would students attend? What would the community, his colleagues, or the school district think about his pledge? The impossibility of answering questions about the future to which the event of obligation guides us – its unanswerability – is the answer to the question. As an event, the obligation to care belongs to a future that none of us can see coming, "over which neither teacher nor student has disposal, what neither one knows or foresees or commands" (Caputo, 2012, p. 29). Obligation calls each of us to do our best "in an impossible situation," that is, "to see what is possible," to "see what comes" (Caputo, 2012, p. 30).

Faith in the unexpected – a teacher's capacity to respond to the alarm bells of obligation, to hope for the best, to make the best of events – is what ultimately provokes and sustains each teacher's singularity as an ethical subject. The teacher's singularity – their irreplaceability and inimitability in particular moments – summons the teacher beyond complacency or disillusionment towards response. There may be no rhyme or reason to what occurs, no *logos* or *telos*. There may only be the question, "What has to be done?" In such moments, one is compelled to follow the pulse of one's passion (Ruti, 2014), rather than rely on routine responses. Justin had to be inventive, caught, as it were, between degrees of freedom and unfreedom; and having to live between contractually defined duties and the promissory relation of the obligation to care (Janzen & Phelan, 2018).

Becoming Politically Conscious

There are kids I'll lose. And when those kids go [i.e., drop out], other kids see that there's a level of despair that's reasonable.

(Ian, high school teacher)

Caring in the context of school is typically focused on institutional priorities – tending to students' basic needs so they can achieve academically (Valenzuela, 1999). In contrast, Matias & Zembylas (2014) posit what they see as a more authentic form of caring as that which is "ideologically wedded to under privileged groups' struggles for equal educational opportunity" (p. 263). We argue that becoming politically conscious, that is, ideologically attached to a political cause, is another example of eccentric care. Paradoxically, this form of care responds to the silent cries of the Other, the ones who cannot speak for themselves.

Consider Ian, a teacher in a large urban high school. There is little doubt that Ian has lost faith in the objective conditions of schooling, as he notes the lack of human and material resources to meet the needs of his non-English-speaking refugee and immigrant students. Teaching is not what he expected. Ian marched alongside his students and their parents when they protested the imminent school closure and ever-dwindling resources for English Language Learning – a deed certainly beyond the commitments of his contract.

As Ian witnesses his colleagues leaving the school to find positions elsewhere, he wonders about the possibilities of a life beyond the school, the district, and the profession. But still he remains. When asked why, Ian answers, "I have a job and I'm paid to do it and I could just stick to it, but I'm with those kids and I know … I can't just walk away from it." He expresses his abiding concern for the children of immigrants and refugees from the school neighbourhood: "[W]hy does the first generation have to completely fail and leave school in grade eleven? There are kids I'll lose. And when those kids go [i.e., drop out], other kids see that there's a level of despair that's reasonable…. I try to … give kids the chance to tell their stories." As Ian describes his students – most of them newcomers to Canada – witnessing their friends and relatives drop out of school, his concern is palpable. He is held captive by their silent cries. As a result of educational cutbacks to English Language Learning (ELL) programs, students are not receiving adequate instruction, and without access to the language of power, their prospects for further academic study or apprenticeships hang in the balance. With so few ELL teachers remaining, Ian wonders, "Who can create … that feeling for a student that adults get where they're coming from and can be relied upon to be on their side?" He witnesses the marginalization of the reality and concerns of his immigrant students, their parents, and the community. Those teachers and school leaders who might have supported them have moved on; policymakers immersed in economic reasoning operate at a distance from any community protestations, and the students' testimony is, "there's no point coming to school." For some teachers the threat of school closure is too much, and they leave to find more secure locations for their work. Others stay, trying, like Ian, to ward off "a kind of terrorism of the soul" (Martuswicz 1997, p. 102) among students.

Here, the singular and silent lament of the newcomer holds the teacher captive; these are high school students newly arrived in Canada who speak little English and whose parents – some refugees, others immigrants – work long hours for minimum wage. In their new context they have become, in a sense, victims, unable to register any complaint about what has and is happening to them;

neither students nor their families have much say in the future of their school or in their own futures. For Ian, each student that drops out of school is heard as a cry that signifies powerlessness: they are *différends* (Lyotard, 1988) – victims because they have been placed "in a position of being unable to show that they have been done a wrong" (Caputo, 1993, p. 164). They must operate in an idiom that cannot and does not signify the wrong they have suffered. As such, their testimony is neutralized.

Through the silence and the feeling of pain that accompanies it, the *différend* confronts the teacher with an obligation not only to testify and redress the wrong but also to institute a new sense of addressee, addressor, and testimony. In being moved by the wrong, the teacher's obligation is reinstated and the possibility of difference and justice along with it. How will parents "defend themselves," Ian asks, in a context in which they are not recognized as addressor nor their testimony taken seriously by those in power? In being moved by the wrongdoing, the teacher's obligation is reinstated and the possibility of difference and justice along with it. Ian encourages his students to walk with him in marches against school closures; parents also join the marches. In between, Ian doubles down on his classroom work with students, cultivating their capacity to tell their stories: "[W]e're trying to hold this together for the kids. We're trying to make this place work because our job is to teach.... So as long as I have that kind of [parental] support, then I think I can do it for another day. If they'll send the kids, I'll stick around." Still, as he witnesses his old department "dwindling and dwindling and dwindling," his school is listed for potential closure. As Caputo (1993) tells us, "disaster happens, i.e., it always happens, always and already, and always will. There is no suggestion that we can put a stop to it, only that we can watch out for it or provide an idiom for its record" (p. 183). In part, Ian's decision to participate in this study provides that record.

Ian's extension of his links to students beyond the classroom and into the community reflects his appreciation of the importance of strong relations between teachers and communities as "a cornerstone of any racially conscious student-teacher caring relationship" (Gallagher, 2016, p. 10). Such care is inexhaustible but always already verges on exhaustion because of its urgency and undecidability (Caputo, 1993). Precisely because the condition of care is "an unconditional and limitless commitment, it is beyond human possibilities, which is to say that when you make the promise to care, you will invariably betray this promise" (p. 168). Whether Ian remains at his school and as deeply engaged as he was when we spoke is unknown to us.

Experiencing Intimacy

Sometimes kids are really destitute.... This kid [Stephen] was hospitalized for ... a suicide attempt. And his parents said "we're done with you. We've had enough of the drama!" So they didn't even go to the hospital to pick him up.... So I [went with] the police, went and picked him up, and uh, took him to a friend's house because his parents said don't, don't bring him home.

(Doug, school counsellor)

Lingis (1994) suggests that there are two entries into communication. One is formulated within rational discourse. Communication between teachers and students, for example, is generally expressed within the terms of the rational discourse wherein one's "visions and insights" are largely "depersonalized" (p. 116). When the teacher speaks or acts as a teacher, they are in effect representatives of the profession – "interchangeable with others." The other entry into communication, Lingis writes, is "that in which you find it is you, you saying something, that is essential" (p. 116). In an encounter between Doug and the student, Stephen, we witness such a moment when it matters more that the teacher "be totally and non-selectively present to the student" as the student addresses the teacher (Noddings, 1984, p. 180). "The time interval may be brief but the encounter total" (p. 180). It is a situation in which *what* is said is far less important than the attempt to say *something*. The experience of "home" is not conveyed through words (language does not have the power to say what has to be said) but by presence, that is, by contact and accompaniment. In fact, as we witnessed in Justin's story, words may appear "vacuous and absurd in one's mouth" (Lingis, 1994, p. 108). Yet, one has to be there, bearing witness, finding something to say or something to do.

Cast out, Stephen becomes known to Doug in a moment haunted by death, homelessness, and the shallow sociality of the crowded high school – where relations are held together by routine, convenience, and duty rather than any real connection (Ruti, 2014). What Stephen seems to need from the teacher is not a kind of care that takes over and does things for the Other, or offers him perspective on his situation, or answers questions he may have about the difficulties he faces. No, what the Other needs in such circumstances is "the contact and the accompaniment" (Lingis, 1994, p. 132). Doug says: "So then he comes to me the next day and he says like, of course he's not going, he's not going to class: 'Well, I have no place to live, and I have no food to eat.' So ... I took him downtown to the shelter and said, 'Well, here's a bed for the night until we figure something out, right?'" No long-term solutions – only the promise that they would figure something out together. Here we witness an "exposed potentiality of living together in a space ungoverned by any economy" (Verwoert, 2009, p. 172); this is care in all its eccentricity. For Doug, being with Stephen in these ways amounts to what he characterized as "breaking his own rules" as a teacher, meaning he abides by a self-imposed imperative to keep an appropriate distance from students – professional limits on caring too much. Bolt (2018) cites the artist Bianca Hester (2014) in this regard: "Leaving a door open provokes a commitment to being responsive no matter what happens to enter and no matter how different or unsettling this may be to the plans that we fashion in advance. In committing to responding, what is affirmed is the willingness to both encounter and grapple with what enters, even if uncertain or radically unprepared" (Hester, 2014, in Bolt, 2018, p. 74). As Stephen not only seeks a home in the literal sense, he may also be seeking home as "a zone of tranquility and warmth and a precinct of intimacy recessed from the uncharted expanses of the alien" (Lingis, 1994, p. 126). He and Doug form "a community of those who have nothing in common" (Lingis, 1994). "Nothingness" in this instance refers to an experience of dispossession and "inner debilitation" (p. 163) wherein all that is anticipated is impossibility. A community of those who have nothing in common offers only *temporary* shelter – a home, if you will – but casts a long shadow of unmet obligation. The student passes on to the next grade or the next school or into life. Teachers don't know what happens to them. Another teacher in our study described her relationship with a suicidal seven-year-old child: "I mean I watched him go through our school and nothing ever really changed. Nothing ever really changed." Teachers like Doug often find themselves forfeiting their professional home, frowned upon by, and increasingly isolated from, colleagues who see their acts of caring as excessive and unprofessional.

While we have little understanding of the value of Doug's actions for Stephen – though we suspect it was significant – the impact of this encounter on Doug compelled him to ask, "what's happening here?" But there is little time to wonder about the failure of the social system, the sheer difficulty of growing up, the challenges of parenting, or of simply staying alive. Rather, Doug is compelled to "lend a hand when the damage threatens to run beyond control, to help restore the possibility of joy, the rhythm of ordinary things" for this vulnerable student (Caputo, 1993, p. 243). There is no room for deliberation.

Ruti (2014) characterizes such moments as involving a "swerve of passion," a sudden upsurge of passion that overpowers, and sometimes even erases, our usual sources of passion" (p. 124). These moments invoke a desire that undoes a conscious desire (Caputo, 1993). Just about to leave school for the day, looking forward to a family birthday celebration or just some time at the local gym, a teacher receives a phone call – maybe from a parent, the police, or a student – calling because they are desperate for help and have nowhere left to turn. The moment is as "terrifying as it is exhilarating" (Ruti, 2014, p. 124).

In each of these aspects of eccentric care, teachers are seen to work across physical, emotional, cognitive, and pedagogical spaces of their professional lives. Each takes on "a level of emotional engagement and political awareness not necessarily expected or even encouraged of teachers" (Gallagher, 2016, p. 28). That said, care always consorts with power, and to this complication we now turn.

Power and Care

Each encounter reflects the reality that the obligation to care occurs in the midst of difficult inheritances – colonization, globalization, neoliberalism – and that it "can make no clean break with the powerful" (Caputo, 1993, p. 173). Lest we believe in the myth that care, however eccentric or excessive, is essentially good, Caputo cautions: "Obligation is always complicitous with systems of power and violence. Obligation inevitably produces violence and perpetuates evils, simply because whoever acts is woven into the texture of the world (*polis*) and implicated in worldly power. Whoever acts, whoever undertakes to meet an obligation, inevitably pulls the strings of power and creates new binds, creating new knots in the act of loosening old ones" (p. 173). Unfurling the knots entangled in our four gestures – being moved and caught off guard, taking a leap of faith, becoming politically conscious, and creating intimacy – is crucial because there is a distinct danger in depoliticizing the eccentricities of care. Eccentricities of care reflect, interrupt, and reinforce historical and political contexts and relations.

Shihmei's story attests to the absence of ethical conditions for international students who are still minors by law, but her story also clarifies "the many competing interests, investments, values and desires that shape school's current form and seek to influence its future direction" (p. 24). The question of internationalization is linked to "long-standing uneven global relations" (Stein, de Oliveira Andreotti, & Suša, 2019, p. 23). Couched in a language of opportunity and equity, Larkin (2015) contends that internationalization of education may simply reproduce Canada's geopolitical hegemony, particularly in the Global South (in Stein, de Oliveira Andreotti, & Suša, 2019, p. 24). The danger is that teachers' responses to students like Linh, the international, homestay student, may at best be the difference that does not make a difference or at worst serve to "reproduce civilizational hierarchies" (p. 26). All international education may be doing is "selectively extracting and consuming difference and inserting it back into existing, dominant frames and horizons of hope" (p. 27).

In reflecting on Justin's story and our own positionality, we consider the "long-standing patterns of power that emerged as a result of colonialism, but that define culture, labor, intersubjective relations, and knowledge production well beyond the strict limits of colonial administrations" (Maldonado-Torres, 2007, p. 243). In Justin's story, we sense our own complicity – and perhaps his own liberal self-positioning – in constructing him as white saviour. One could ask, will expanding the drama program do little more than reproduce Westernized versions of being and knowing? While this depiction does not do credit to Justin's humility and his earnest efforts to collaborate with students and community members, we recognize that, like Justin, we too live and work on stolen lands – whether under legal agreement or unceded – reinforcing settler-colonial foundations, epistemology and ontology, in our teaching and research.

Neoliberal social and funding policies, outlined in the Introduction to this volume, set the stage for Ian's efforts to recognize the different social contexts of home and school, to invite his students to tell their very particular stories, and to engage politically with the school community to prevent the school from closing – all "emotionally draining and time-consuming work" (Gallagher, 2016, p. 30) that diminishes the distance between home and school, but which continues to reinforce English as the language of power. The teacher's own embodiment of the dominant idiom of English speaks volumes and it exploits the students' desire to be recognizable as Canadian, reinforcing their dependence on English and maintaining its power.

Even Doug's encounter with Stephen raises the issue of learned dependency. As Caputo (1993) advises: "Lending a hand to others is a way of inducing dependence and of reducing them to subservience. That is something we cannot help; it is built in. We inevitably produce new evils in trying to solve existing ones" (p. 174). Of course, this cannot be a teacher's excuse not to act, not to do whatever one can – that would be absurd. As Caputo reminds us, "The imperative to act, the power of obligation, is urgent, incessant" (p. 174). Because care consorts with the powerful, teachers like Shihmei, Doug, Justin, and Ian are left fighting with shadows; while the suffering of others matters, there is no warranty against teachers doing more harm. The good is at best the lesser evil. Moreover, the long-range ends remain unknown (Caputo, 1993).

Conclusion

There is a kind of madness at play in the teaching lives of Justin, Ian, Doug, and Shihmei. A necessary madness – a suffering, if you will – that the discourse of teachers' mental health may silence in its attempt to make meaning and contain feeling, thereby quietening the incessant roar of obligation that characterizes some teaching lives. Some discourses of teachers' mental health and well-being are about keeping teachers upright, reasserting their uprightness versus attempting to appreciate the potentiality of inclination.

We are not writing here about all teachers or about all schools; our claims are far more modest and at the same time, in some sense, a little more excessive. Our purpose here has been simply to record that eccentricities of care happen in schools, to remark upon their remarkable quality, to acknowledge that becoming touched, being foolish, or even a little mad may be the greatest source of a teacher's sensitive and sensuous sanity.

References

Bingham, C., & Sidorkin, A.M. (2004). *No education without relation*. Peter Lang.

Bolt, B. (2018). Couch grass: Ethics of the rhizome. In C. Åsberg & R. Braidotti (Eds.), *A feminist companion to the posthumanities* (pp. 67–80). Springer.

Caputo, J.D. (1993). *Against ethics: Contributions to a poetics of obligation with constant reference to deconstruction*. Indiana University Press.

– (2012). Teaching the event: Deconstruction, hauntology, and the scene of pedagogy. In C.W. Ruitenberg (Ed.), *Philosophy of education yearbook* (pp. 23–34). Philosophy of Education Society.

Connell, R. (2009). Good teachers on dangerous ground: Toward a new view of teacher quality and professionalism. *Critical Studies in Education, 50*(3), 213–29. https://doi.org/10.1080/17508480902998421

Elnagar, A., & Young, J. (2021). International education and the internationalization of public schooling in Canada: Approaches and conceptualizations. *Canadian Journal of Educational Administration and Policy/ Revue Canadienne en Administration et Politique de l'Éducation(195)*, 80–94. https://doi.org/10.7202/1075674ar

Gallagher, K. (2016). Can a classroom be a family? Race, space, and the labour of care in urban. *Canadian Journal of Education, 39*(2): 1–36.

Hester, B. (2014). Please leave these windows open overnight to enable the fans to draw in cool air during the early hours of the morning. Australian Centre for Contemporary Art.

Janzen, M., & Phelan, A.M. (2018). 'Tugging at our sleeves': Understanding experiences of obligation in teaching. *Teaching Education*. https://doi.org/10.1080/10476210.2017.1420157

– (September 2020). Battling bad feelings: Understanding the emotional toll of teaching. *Education Canada*. https://www.edcan.ca/articles/battling-bad-feelings/

Jung, J.H. (2015). *Self-care and care-for-others in education*. [Unpublished Doctoral Dissertation]. University of British Columbia, Canada.

Larkin, A. (2015). North-South partnerships in Canadian higher education. In A.A. Abdi (Ed.), *Decolonizing Global Citizenship Education* (pp. 141–55). Sense Publishers.

Lingis, A. (1994). *The Community of those who have nothing in common*. Indiana University Press.

Lyotard, J.-F. (1988). *The differend: Phrases in dispute*. University of Minnesota Press.

Maldonado-Torres, N. (2007). On the coloniality of being. *Cultural Studies, 21*(2), 240–70. https://doi.org/10.1080/09502380601162548

Marko, K.A. (2015). *Hearing the unheard voices: An in-depth look at teacher mental health and wellness*. Electronic Thesis and Dissertation Repository. 2804. https://ir.lib.uwo.ca/etd/2804.

Martuswicz, R. (1997). Say me to me. In S. Todd (Ed.), *Learning desire: Perspectives on pedagogy, culture and the unsaid* (pp. 97–113). Routledge.

Matias, C.E., & Zembylas, M. (2014). 'When saying you care is not really caring': Emotions of disgust, whiteness ideology, and teacher education. *Critical Studies in Education, 55*(3), 319–37. https://doi.org/10.1080/17508487.2014.922489

Noddings, N. (1984). Caring: A relational approach to ethics and moral education. University of California Press.

– (2012). The language of care ethics. *Knowledge Quest, 40*(4), 52–6.

Ruti, M. (2014). *The call of character: Living a life worth living*. Columbia University Press.

– (2018). *Penis envy and other bad feelings: The emotional cost of everyday life*. Columbia University Press.

Stein, S., de Oliveira Andreotti, V., & Suša, R. (2019). Pluralizing frameworks for global ethics in the internationalization of higher education in Canada. *Canadian Journal of Higher Education, 49*(1), 22–46. https://doi.org/10.47678/cjhe.v49i1.188244

Valenzuela, A. (1999). *Subtractive schooling: U.S.–Mexican youth and the politics of caring*. The State University of New York Press.

van Manen, M. (1994). Pedagogy, virtue, and narrative identity in teaching. *Curriculum Inquiry*, *24*(2): 135–70. (Summer). https://doi.org/10.1080/03626784.1994.11076157

– (2012). The call of pedagogy as the call of contact. *Phenomenology & Practice*, *6*(2), 8–34. https://doi.org/10.29173/pandpr19859

Verwoert, J. (2009). Personal support: How to care? In C. Condorelli (Ed.), *Support Structures* (pp. 162–72). Sternberg Press.

Chapter 5

Fears and Frustrations: Acknowledging Desire

[T]here's this mountain ahead of you that you've got to climb and everybody on the way up needs something from you.

– Stacey, elementary school teacher

Stacey was a young and enthusiastic participant in our study, and although she often expressed her desire to support, care for, love, and advocate for children, she also expressed her fears and frustrations of failing to fulfil the needs of others. In her attempts to control the uncontrollable and to suppress her worries, Stacey described "always over-planning, overthinking, and wanting to be prepared for anything." Stacey was continually fending off her fears, pushing them to the margins of her thoughts and daily activities. Yet, seemingly stored in her unconscious, her fears were exposed in a bad dream: "I had lots of horrible dreams that related to school shootings and stuff, but in the one dream, this parent came in with a gun, and I was with the kids and so, in the moment, the best thing I could do was just ask that I be taken out of the room to be shot so that the kids didn't have to see it. That was a dream I had a couple of times." Stacey's disturbing dream – a nightmare, really – is a poignant illustration of the ways in which teaching demands too much of the teacher. The dream is a metaphor for the teacher's experience: enacting the necessity of self-sacrifice, caught between the relentless expectations of others while always obligated to the needs of the students. This tension illustrates the affective conflicts experienced by the teacher while also illustrating the effects of obligation, foregrounded in the teacher's fears and frustrations.

According to Deborah Britzman (2006), Freud would call Stacey's dream a "typical dream," where the dreamer is uneasy, a crowd is present and usually unconcerned, and the dream contains an exaggeration.

What typical dreams reflect are three affective conflicts, specifically, "the burden of responsibility, the worry of failing to meet this responsibility and the expectation of and need for punishment" (p. 136). Psychoanalytically speaking, Stacey's dream is a recognizable – yet ordinary – refrain that reflects one's moral anxiety. The dream illustrates what Britzman (2006) calls the "normal, typical expressions of a teacher's life" (p. 128). In Stacey's stories, we see the teacher's frustration arising from a desire to fulfil her responsibilities, her fear of failing to do so, and the anxiety associated with that anticipated failure. In this chapter, we explore the teacher's sense of obligation through the teacher's often extolled experiences of fear and frustration, using the framework of the affective accounts of a dream. In doing so, we will illustrate the ways in which the teacher's desire to be a "good" teacher is in constant tension with the demands of others, including the anxiety of obligation to students.

The Burden of Responsibility

Stacey's stories conveyed the psychic webwork of desire, fear, and frustration – negotiating her own desires with the material demands of others, alongside the constant sense of obligation to students (the pull to respond to students regardless of circumstances). Stacey described this burden of responsibility: "I always feel responsible. Umm, I feel responsible certainly for all the kids and for their behaviours and their moods and their well-being and their happiness and everything. And I feel responsible even when they're not with me, so if they're at recess or if they're at lunch in the classroom and I'm in a meeting or something I feel responsible for what happens." To be responsible, as Sharon Todd (2003) explains, is to not just be concerned for the other, but to achieve "a committed regard for the other that has the potential to lead to responsibility and hopefully responsible action" (p. 66). Understood in this way, responsibility has a spontaneous affect in that it induces emotion; and although one could avoid responding to the demands of the other, the burden of the sense of responsibility cannot be eluded. In fact, it is inescapable (p. 141). Moreover, consistent with a Levinasian understanding, Todd explains that responsibility cannot be prescribed in institutional procedures or teacher codes of conduct; rather, responsibility lies in the surprises and encounters with difference. This means that one's sense of responsibility is derived not from within the subject, but rather it is "something that come[s] to the subject from the other" (p. 106). Responsibility is an ethical encounter with the Other, in which the subject is constituted.

However, we see in Stacey's account of "being responsible for everything" a blurring of responsibility with *responsibilization* (McLeod, 2017). Responsibilization is the requirement that teachers take greater responsibility for the *management* of schooling and of children as a technical and regulatory event rather than as an ethical one. The demands of school make it so that Stacey reported feeling responsible for educational assistants, the decisions of her principal, and "carrying her weight." Here, the expectation of the teacher's responsibilization increases pressures on the teacher, reinforces regulation (of the teacher and of the student), and increases her sense of individualism – that she carries the burden of responsibilization alone. The effects and demands of responsibilization reduce teaching to the management of systems, students, and the self, which have increased in the neoliberal era and have greatly influenced the expectations of what it means to be a "good teacher."

Images of the "good teacher," as conceptualized by Britzman (1986; 2003) have long been influenced by commonly held assumptions of schooling where schooling reflects forms of social control, compartmentalizes curriculum, and reinforces hierarchical authority. These images of the good teacher construct a mythical version of the teacher, as "autonomous, charismatic and in control" (Britzman, 1986, p. 445), thereby glorifying the individual, disregarding structural and material realities, and ignoring the uncertainty of the teacher's world. Moreover, these images of the good teacher are discursive, circulating as norms and constituting the teaching subject (Butler, 1993) – affecting the teacher's understanding of who she is, but also delimitating who she is allowed to be (Janzen, 2015). In this neoliberal era of education reform, where policy technologies of marketization and managerialism permeate education systems, the demands for teachers to enact greater responsibilization create a mode of teacher performativity (Ball, 2003). This increases the teacher's sense of surveillance and of being constantly judged. These multiple demands (of others, of systems, of reform), creates a kaleidoscopic image of the "good teacher" – a fluctuating refraction unstable in time and form, reflecting the teacher's anxiety. The intensity of these demands is evident in Stacey's description of her "normal school week": "there's an overwhelming anxiety – it kind of comes over and I don't feel well. And I feel like I'm not sleeping and then I don't often have time to eat. Drinking water is like a luxury, and if you have time to go to the bathroom, that's amazing. It just feels like, I think physically and mentally you have nothing left to give, but there's this mountain ahead of you that you've got to climb and everybody on the way up needs something from you." Stacey's descriptions of the constant demands being placed on her at the expense of her basic needs creates the sense of utter depletion – a teacher wholly consumed and burdened by the task of teaching.

The incessant demands of others often ignore an understanding of teaching as a relational activity, as "intensely personal, invariably complex, and inevitably unpredictable" (Reid, 2019, p. 722). For Stacey, this too created a burden – one that can be overwhelming in its emotional ramifications and intensified by the fact that this aspiration of teaching can never be realized. In fact, Stacey shared that she "went through a few years where I didn't know if I could do this job." However, Stacey persisted, claiming to have held on to her "passion for teaching" and her efforts to be "an innovative and creative and fun teacher" whom her students "would remember." As Ruti (2009) explains, however, these desires to be good and to be seen as good risk becoming narcissistic fantasies (p. 101), reliant on a psychic idealism that renders identities as coherent and knowable. And so these desires always generate a sense of failure – a sense of lack. This lack denotes an impossible fulfilment that resides within the subject.

The subject's desire – the wanting of what one cannot have – is an "(as yet) unattained ideal" (Ruti, 2014, p. 13), often impossible to attain because they can be "overrun by social norms to such an extent that our desire gets swallowed up" (Ruti, 2014, p. 13). When desire is swallowed up, it becomes frustrated – frustrated by too many actors in the scene: principals, educational professionals, students, parents, the public, and others, all performing from different scripts, each player wanting the impossible from the other (Phillips, 2012). This is the burden of responsibility and the impossibility of satisfying desire; there are too many competing forces (both the external forces and her own unrealizable desires) to satisfy the expectations to be the good teacher. The public nature of teaching and the technologies of performativity (Ball, 2003) – or modes of regulation – create a sense for Stacey that she is always being judged, increasing her self-doubt and feelings of anxiety. Yet, as Ruti (2014) explains, desire is also necessary, understood as "absolutely indispensable for the augmentation of our character" (p. 8). In giving verve to her ideals, Stacey's desire to become a particular teacher invigorates the meaningfulness of her work.

The Fear of Failing to Meet One's Responsibilities

The teacher's relationships with others are often an unrealistic wanting – a perennial affect of unfulfilled desires, entanglements of fear, and persistent frustrations. This frustration arises from the "buildup of expectations or the psychic energy that is not satisfied or has no outlet" (Oliver,

2001, p. 196). The frustration experienced and coupled with the teacher's sense of obligation to students, can have profoundly negative effects on teachers like Stacey, engendering "bad feelings" (Ruti, 2018) of anxiety and self-doubt – and arousing bad dreams. Although Stacey professed that she felt fairly secure in her practices as a teacher at this point in her career – having taught various grades over six years – and was committed to supporting her students, she still encountered scenarios that undermined and challenged her, inciting fear about failing to meet her responsibilities and conveying her frustrations in attempting to do so.

In one such event, Stacey discovered entries in one of her student's notebooks about suicide and self-harm. Naturally, Stacey expressed being "worried about her [the student, Destiny] and trying to figure out my next steps with her." It is a moment that described Stacey's obligation to the other: the demand to respond yet unsure how best to proceed. Stacey described feeling "anxious" and recalled asking herself, "How am I going to be the most professional person and do this the right way?" Stacey knew that she needed advice from her principal and because he was not in the school that day, she sought out guidance from a member of the school's student services team. Stacey was surprised by the response she received: "'Don't address this. Don't address this with the mom. Just leave it.'" Stacey was stunned and stated, "That did not sit well with me. And I felt like … I felt like I had to do more." Although Stacey was directed against it, she shared what she found in Destiny's notebook with Destiny's mother. The following day, Stacey updated the principal on the events, to which the principal flatly responded that Stacey's duties had been fulfilled. According to Stacey, the principal stated, "We've told the mom, so that's all we need to do." Again, Stacey was dismayed by the lack of greater concern and the seemingly negligent response:

> I felt like I was crazy? Was it me? I, I, felt a lot of things, but I didn't know what else to do. I felt like we needed to do something else. There was no follow up…. And then, I just, I just watched Destiny like a hawk. And that was hard too, because I was so conflicted, because I, I definitely felt that the student services [person] wasn't right and the principal was hesitant to deal with it himself…. But it just … it made me really sad and really frustrated because then, I just, I was just so scared for her all the time.

Stacey's response included a frenzied array of unsatisfied emotions, including feeling crazy, surprised, conflicted, sad, frustrated, and scared.

In part, the source of Stacey's frustration was the lack of action from the professional others. She expressed exasperation: "I couldn't believe that that was it!" She was certain that more was required, that more was possible, and yet she felt that whatever "it" was, was being withheld. It was Stacey's wanting of something that she could not have that resulted in her frustration. As Phillips (2012) explains, to feel frustrated is due in some part because one feels deceived, as though someone has something that they are concealing from you. To be frustrated in this way, according to Phillips (2012), "is to be maddened by having ones' demands negated or avoided … it is as though a contract has been broken" (p. 10). Stacey was indeed maddened and felt deprived of something – more help for a desperate girl – that she believed was entirely feasible and, in fact, necessary.

Stacey's frustration illustrates her belief that more could have been done to support Destiny. Yet, one wonders, what is the "more" that Stacey sought? What "supports" might be a satisfactory response for a desperate, and perhaps even suicidal, child? There is an assumption in Stacey's desire that what she *wants* actually *exists*; as if there is a sufficient reply or a prescribed remedy for such emotional distress – and that someone knows it and can administer it. Yet, Stacey hoped, "I felt like we needed to do something else." Perhaps Stacey's frustration with her unsatisfied desires for Destiny reflects an optimism (Phillips, 2012) – a belief that there actually is an adequate response that would guide Destiny out of her desolation. Stacey's gesture towards an "as if" demonstrated a faith in what could – or what should – be possible, revealing an unfettered optimism that says, "surely, we can do better." These moments of hope – the desire for future-oriented possibilities – not only imagine something better for the child, but also invigorate and sustain the work of teaching (Birmingham, 2009).

These moments of fear and frustration activate the teacher's responsibility – her concern for the Other – as we see in another of Stacey's stories, this time concerning the mistreatment of a student, Elijah, by another teacher. According to Stacey, "Elijah was being rude, which is totally a problem, but the teacher said something like, 'if you keep this up you're going to find yourself dead in an alley because nobody likes kids who say things like that!'" Stacey was furious and said: "Oooh! When I heard about that, I went to my principal and that was tough because that was the only time I didn't follow the professional code of going to the teacher first, but a child's welfare is at stake, and so, yeah, I definitely had to be his advocate!" In Stacey's efforts to protest the mistreatment of and protect her student, she felt forced to call out her colleague, illustrating not only her sense of responsibility towards her student, but also perhaps to herself – responding to her desires to be the good teacher. As Birmingham (2009) indicates, "In the lived experience of teaching, hope for oneself is essentially tied to hope for one's students" (p. 31). Thus, in making a complaint to her principal, Stacey attempts to enact a particular identity of a good teacher, illustrating an effort to mitigate "the distance between who I feel myself to be and who I want to be" (Phillips, 2012, p. 146). It is in eruption of the frustration with her colleague's conduct that Stacey signals both her desire for this (unachievable) ideal of the good teacher, as well as her fear of failing to attain it.

Phillips (2012) explains that in Stacey's desire to be good and in calling out her colleague, she also projected her ideal onto others. These frustrations illuminate moments of transformation, where "we would rather destroy everything than let other people change us" (Phillips, 2012, p. 10). In resisting being changed, Stacey held this ideal of the good teacher as not only her own aspiration but operationalized it as a universalized standard to which she expected others to be held. Stacey expected more from her colleague, and he failed to live up. In this move, we see how frustration becomes a "temptation scene" (Phillips, 2012, p. 13) luring us to seek solutions that uphold "radical self-deceptions" (p. 13) of ourselves – as well as of others. Stacey's desire becomes a temptation that ultimately (and inevitably) results in frustration. It is a deception in which she endeavoured to change herself and her colleague, expecting that they could both be or become good teachers – teachers who are more than simply flawed humans in complex relations with often vulnerable others.

Stacey's frustration helps us to appreciate what is good about her bad feelings, specifically the ways in which frustration provokes us to "imagine – to elaborate, to envision – our desire" (Phillips, 2012, p. xx). We see in Stacey's stories how frustration can be the moment where lack is identified in the first place and then how the experience of frustration impels a *thinking* about mitigating that frustration through hope. Frustration might be helpful in imagining the potential – of what might be differently, or in thinking about what is possible (Phillips, 2012). Stacey's frustration animates her desire for her students to feel "loved" and "cared for," her hope for their future, and the potential to live out one's own subjectivity. Although the teacher harbours desire to do better for children – a desire that can never be fulfilled exactly as imagined and so is always frustrated – it is the teacher's frustration that illustrates this "dawning of a need" (Phillips, 2012, p. 26). In this circuitous – and perhaps somewhat slippery way – Phillips explains that bearing frustrations reveals for us the teacher's "struggles for satisfaction" (p. 27). This struggle complicates the teacher's perception of obligation and her capacity to respond, highlighting the teacher's desire that is always at risk of being frustrated.

Being Bad and the Expectation of Punishment

The impossible demands of others and the internalized sense of responsibilization instil in teachers like Stacey a fear of being not good enough, of being deemed "bad," and ultimately, of being punished. Being deemed a bad teacher can affect the teacher's reputation within her current standing and relationships within the school and community, within the profession, and in regard to her future career. Stacey described this fear as being more prominent when she first started teaching, explaining: "So, I, I was very fearful that I was going to have a bad name in the [school] division or that I would have a bad name as a teacher, like if somehow, something was said that uhm, that I didn't have a chance to kind of explain or to, be aware of before other people heard." The problem, as we have noted, is that the good teacher is a shifting, elusive, and at times, even an undesirable construct. For example, neoliberal attempts to responsibilize the teacher demand rationality, calculability, and instrumentality (McWilliam, 2008). This kind of good teacher, formulaic and certain, represents the "wishful fantasies of satisfaction" (Phillips, 2012, p. 150). In such fantasies, the sterile and standardized teacher exacts the "imaginary monsters of our lives" (Ruti, 2009, p. 57), amplifying self-scrutiny as well as the perception of being constantly scrutinized by others. It creates a sense of constant fear of punishment in that the teacher strives – and fails – to be recognizable as the good teacher, while also risking being recognizable to herself. These (imaginary?) monsters are what scare the teacher, evoking anxiety about being exposed as "bad" and as being subject to the subsequent and inevitable reprimand.

These monsters crept into Stacey's bad dream described earlier: a terrifying parent who stormed into Stacey's classroom with the intention of shooting her. There is something telling that this monster takes the form of a parent – as possibly every parent to whom Stacey feels she must console, conform, and oblige. To refute the demands of parents is risky – and scarier for newer teachers especially. Although we never asked teachers about parents directly in our interviews, Stacey (like all teachers we interviewed) conveyed her fears of parents on numerous occasions, saying, "I'm constantly worried – I'm worried [about parents]." Then, a few minutes later, she said: "Sometimes in parent meetings I feel fearful, just more that I'll, that I'll feel uhm, like they'll ask me a question that I hadn't planned well enough. So that's why I'm always over planning or always over thinking because I just always want to be prepared for anything that comes my way." We hear in Stacey's concern her attempts to control the muddle of living together in schools – as if the events of this existence could be planned for and controlled in advance.

Stacey's concerns of not-enoughness produce a hot house of anxiety and stoke her fears of being punished. Stacey said, "I feel responsible for everything. I feel like ultimately everything comes down to me." So even when Stacey's principal told her that her duties to Destiny were fulfilled, she simply could not walk away. This sense of being "responsible for everything" reflects the tensions between the internalized sense of responsibilization (McLeod, 2017) and the obligation of responding to the Other. Importantly, the responsibilization of teaching is premised on gendered stereotypes of the teacher. Teaching has long been considered women's work, characterized as emotional labour, and relegated to the domestic, private sphere, like the home (Grumet, 1988; Prentice & Theobald, 1991). Thus, teachers' protestations about the conditions of their work are often dismissed as complaints, and in particular, "female complaints," fuelled by gendered stereotypes of teachers as emotional, irrational, and even hysterical – allowing the complaint to be dismissed and delegitimized (Berlant, 1988). Stacey can complain to the principal about the lack of response for Destiny or the inappropriate treatment of Elijah, but these are easily disregarded. The "complaining" teacher can be ignored in political arenas and the teacher's complaint is seen as being bad – even *irresponsible* – in that these complaints disavow the expectations of responsibilization. Just as the good teacher remains an elusive aspiration, it is especially difficult – impossible, even – to be the good *female* teacher (McWilliam, 1996).

At one point, Stacey sighed and said, "So you really can't win. So, I always end up feeling – I feel guilty for not doing something or for doing something or – yeah.... So yes, I feel guilty." Her daily reality, as in her bad dream, is awash in a fear of failing and fear of punishment – and at the same time, continuing to blame herself for these fears. As Britzman (2006) explains, the anxiety that surfaces in Stacey's bad dream is not a fear of something that might happen; it represents the fears that are happening and that *have happened* – the worst has already occurred! In other words, the fear of being punished is both an anxiety of an anticipated punishment but is also a punishment that has already befallen. Stacey – like all teachers – have *always already* failed at being the good (responsibilized) teacher. Stacey feels responsible for everything and in a way, consumes – and punishes – herself.

These fears and frustrations, bad feelings and bad dreams, and anxieties of failing everyone are reflective of the everyday experience of teaching and represent the impossible desires and "the tragedy of everyday life" (Phillips, 2012, p. 33). They are indeed the tragedy of teaching.

Everyone is left wanting, each player harbouring desires impossible for the other to fulfil; the students need more, the parents want the impossible, the public expects everything, and the teacher fails to deliver. These fears and frustrations are the symptoms of the teacher's illness (Britzman, 2006) and represent the "radical uncertainty of being with others" (Britzman, 2009, p. 27). It is the human and relational qualities of teaching that make the work of teaching impossible to standardize, measure, and quantify, and perhaps why Freud (1937) deemed teaching an "impossible profession." It is within this understanding that we see the impossibility of being the good teacher, and with its enduring emotionality, we seek instead to understand what it means to be good-enough.

The Good-Enough Teacher

To seek an understanding of the "good-enough" teacher is not to imply a low bar of acceptability or of mediocrity, as if the teacher needs only to be adequate. Rather, we are drawing on a psychoanalytic concept of the "good-enough" mother first advanced by the British psychoanalyst D. W. Winnicott in the 1950s and used as a metaphor for any caregiver of the child. For Winnicott, the notion of the good-enough mother was one in which the mother is adaptive to the infant's needs, providing both illusion (when the child has her wants and needs met) and disillusionment (when the child is frustrated by not getting what she wants, similar to weaning). It is in disillusionment that the child begins to relate to the realities of – and develop a relationship with – the world (Winnicott, 2005/1971). Being a good-enough mother means revising one's responses and helping the child to develop a capacity for illusion and disillusionment so that the child can tolerate misunderstandings of – and being misunderstood by – the world. To be a good-enough mother is meant to disrupt the notion of the perfect mother, a recognition that there is no flawless formula or fixed ideal. In fact, it is devotion, as a quality of the relational experience, that defines good-enough mothering; premised not on a standardized or scripted formula seeking perfection, but rather on a relationship that requires judgment and, subsequently, is accompanied by doubt (Reid, 2019).

Similarly, the good-enough teacher, as conceptualized by Britzman (1998), is key in fostering the student's capacity for illusion and disillusion. "The 'good enough' teacher must also help herself in tolerating the results of her or his own frustration" (Britzman, 1998, p. 42). To be a good-enough teacher is to understand that teaching is not an activity of perfected lesson plans or of predefined outcomes, but rather to render teaching as "at once intensely personal, invariably complex, and inevitably unpredictable" (Reid, 2019, p. 722). Like the good-enough mother, there is no script to work from. As we see with Stacey, test scores, teaching standards, or prescribed curriculum could not have determined her responses to – nor would have helped – Destiny or Elijah. As we have illustrated, no matter the response, frustration is likely to ensue, illustrating both a voracious hope and an unrealistic desire.

In Stacey's responses to the obligations of students, Stacey experiences a momentary "flight from wanting; a refuge from the rigours and risks of desire" (Phillips, 2012, p. 139). Stacey's brief satisfaction in responding to the needs of the child, in identifying as an advocate, for example, allow for a momentary sanctuary from the frustration created by the unbearability of the constant and inextricable wanting of more for students. These brief moments of satisfaction must be good-enough – for there is nothing more to come. As Ruti (2009) instructs, "Our task in other words, is to learn to endure the sharp points of existence without being devastated by them" (p. 103). The sharp points of the teacher's existence – her fears and frustrations – reflect the teacher's human experience, the ways in which these affects are a "precondition to becoming" (Ruti, 2018). As we see with Stacey, the teacher's fears and frustrations reflect the qualities of obligation – a psychic pulse of blurred energy that receives no satisfaction, except perhaps in knowing that the good teacher can only ever be good-enough.

References

Ball, S. J. (2003). The teacher's soul and the terrors of performativity. *Journal of Education Policy, 18*(2), 215–28. https://doi.org/10.1080/0268093022000043065

Berlant, L. (1988). The female complaint. *Social Text, 19/20*, 237–59. https://doi.org/10.2307/466188

Birmingham, C. (2009). The disposition of hope in teaching. *Teacher Education Quarterly, 36*(4), 27–39.

Britzman, D. (1986). Cultural myths in the making of a teacher: Biography and social structure in teacher education. *Harvard Educational Review, 56*(4), 442–57. https://doi.org/10.17763/haer.56.4.mv28227614l44u66

– (1998). *Lost subjects, contested objects: Toward a psychoanalytic inquiry of learning*. The State University of New York Press.

– (2003). *Practice makes practice: A critical study of learning to teach* (rev. ed.). The State University of New York Press.

– (2006). *Novel education: Psychoanalytic studies of learning and not learning*. Peter Lang.

– (2009). *The very though of education: Psychoanalysis and the impossible profession*. The State University of New York Press.
Butler, J. (1993). *Bodies that matter: On the discursive limits of sex*. Routledge.
Freud, S. (1937). Analysis terminable and interminable. *The International Journal of Psychoanalysis, 18*, 373–405.
Grumet, M.R. (1988). *Bitter milk: Women and teaching*. University of Massachusetts Press.
Janzen, M.D. (2015). "Free yourself, sister!": Teacher identity, subjection, and the psyche. *Asia-Pacific Journal of Teacher Education, 43*(2), 117–27. https://doi.org/10.1080/1359866x.2014.933472
McLeod, J. (2017). Reframing responsibility in an era of responsibilisation: Education, feminist ethics. *Discourse: Studies in the Cultural Politics of Education, 38*(1), 43–56. https://doi.org/10.1080/01596306.2015.1104851
McWilliam, E. (1996). Seductress or schoolmarm: On the improbability of the great female teacher. *Interchange, 27*(1), 1–11. https://doi.org/10.1007/bf01807481
– (2008). Making excellent teachers. In A. Phelan & J. Sumsion (Eds.), *Critical readings in teacher education: Provoking absences* (pp. 33–44). Sense Publishers.
Oliver, K. (2001). *Witnessing: Beyond recognition*. University of Minnesota Press.
Phillips, A. (2012). *Missing out: In praise of the unlived life*. Picador.
Prentice, A.L., & Theobald, M.R. (Eds.). (1991). *Women who taught: Perspectives on the history of women and teaching*. University of Toronto Press.
Reid, J.-A. (2019). What's good enough? Teacher education and the practice challenge. *The Australian Educational Researcher, 46*(5), 715–34. https://doi.org/10.1007/s13384-019-00348-w
Ruti, M. (2009). *A world of fragile things: Psychoanalysis and the art of living*. The State University of New York Press.
– (2014). *The call of character: Living a life worth living*. Columbia University Press.
– (2018). *Penis envy and other bad feelings: The emotional costs of everyday life*. Columbia University Press.
Todd, S. (2003). *Learning from the other: Levinas, psychoanalysis, and ethical possibilities in education*. The State University of New York Press.
Winnicott, D.W. (2005). *Playing and reality*. Routledge. (Original work published 1971)

Chapter 6

Revitalizing Teaching as Vocation

A Return to Miserable Conditions

What does teaching do to teachers in these times? Our interest in this question initially stemmed from a story about Patricia, an experienced grade one teacher, and her student Devan. Frequently violent and uncontrollable, Devan has to be physically restrained until calm. In such moments, Patricia calls the school office to send help. No one ever comes. Feeling shaken after each of these episodes, she worries about her distressed relationship with Devan and about what the other children think when they witness such scenes. She worries about the safety of the students, the lack of support for Devan's family, how the other teachers and the principal judge her, and the curriculum that isn't being taught. One afternoon, Patricia is rushed to hospital with chest pains. The diagnosis: badly bruised ribs, the result of Devan's head banging against her chest while being restrained. The prognosis: immediate stress leave, followed by Patricia's decision to leave the profession altogether. When asked about her motives for leaving, Patricia cites "personal reasons" and "job dissatisfaction." Devan and his classmates finish the year with a variety of substitute teachers and then two different term contract teachers.

What struck us forcibly about this teacher's story is that Devan, a child growing up in Canada in the twenty-first century, is so under-valued that neither he nor his family receive sufficient supports to ensure his educational well-being. As a result, the emotional and physical labour required of his teacher is unsustainable (Connell, 2009). It is not insignificant that teachers, like Patricia, who leave the profession do so in greatest numbers in schools with vulnerable populations, such as children from families with low socio-economic status (Kersaint, Lewis, Potter, & Meisels, 2007), or minority students (Borman & Kimball, 2005; Ferguson, 1998; Kain & Singleton, 1996). It is in such schools that "a felt erosion of concern" (Greene, 1988, p. 476) on the part of policymakers is most profound. Consequently, when teachers leave, it negatively impacts students for whom teachers' emotional commitment is a critical factor in their academic success and well-being (Crocco & Costigan, 2007; Day & Gu, 2010; Loeb, Darling-Hammond, & Luczak, 2005; Steeves, Carr-Stewart, Kirk, & Prytula, 2013). Therefore, as particular school children bear the brunt of society's injustices disproportionately, and as Canadian classrooms are becoming more complex (greater diversity of cultures, languages, and abilities; children living in poverty; youth struggling with issues of mental health), ethical obligation threatens to overwhelm teachers – as it did Patricia – risking greater attrition, and ultimately negatively impacting the very children who need engaged teachers the most.

While the issues associated with attrition are significant, our interest in this research study focused on the emotional toll of obligation felt by those teachers who remained in teaching. As the preceding chapters attest, the majority of the teachers in the study expressed a deep ambivalence about staying in teaching but they <u>did</u> stay. Much can be learned by attending to the stories of those who remained – Lena, Doug, Ian, and Justin, among others – about the conditions in which they worked, how teaching impacted them, and what enabled them to endure with integrity.

The working conditions for teachers in this study were largely influenced by neoliberalism and its sister financialization, whereby finance capital (future-oriented growth) is privileged over productive capital (labour and current profits) (Brown, 2017; Fraser, 2016). Within the educational sphere, financialization manifests as the future valuation of some children and youth – those who increase or maintain their performance ratings – and the devaluing of those perceived as having no future value.

Expressions of the future-valuation of children have become ubiquitous in political speeches, including at international venues, such as the United Nations, where Sam Kutesa, president of the 69th Session of the General Assembly stated, "the more young people grow into well-educated adults with fewer dependents and new opportunities to acquire wealth, savings and purchasing power, the more they will be able to accelerate economic growth and development" (United Nations, 1 June 2015). While we are not arguing that young people do not deserve bright futures, what we do oppose is the positioning of youth as future producers of wealth and consumers of goods and the limiting of children's "worth" to economic and future-oriented terms.

Many parents have succumbed to neoliberal ideals of economization, monetization, and financialization in the ways in which they understand the role of school. Parker (2017) exposes how, in the province of Ontario, neoliberal education policies, often without any evidentiary basis, came to be endorsed via savvy marketing strategies. Politicians "rebranded" education through the rhetoric of crisis; asserting that students were falling behind international peers and forecasting Ontario's economic demise, and then making, communicating (via speeches and public debates, television and newspaper reports), and delivering on promises of accountability. The curriculum of accountability – increased power for principals, more authority for the ministry, and standardized testing to hold teachers accountable for student achievement – persisted through several governments, beginning with the New Democratic Party (1993), extended by the Progressive Conservative Party (1995), and then by the Liberal Party (2003). The paths followed by British Columbia and Manitoba are similar to that of Ontario. In British Columbia, for example, the provincial government has been administering the Foundation Skills Assessment (FSA) test to all students in grades four and seven since 2000. Like all such assessments, this test does not help students learn or teachers teach. It takes valuable time and much-needed resources away from the classroom learning and undermines the ability to provide meaningful learning experiences for all students (British Columbia Teachers' Federation, 2021).

Education systems that continue to invest in testing, standardization, and accountability measures might serve to underscore and validate parents' concerns; however, those concerns have been manufactured by governments in the first instance (Parker, 2017). Governments follow the same strategy: decry a crisis of school failure, blame the teachers for said failure, and then promise improvement through neoliberal reforms (Klees, 2020). Reduced to standardized testing and developmental assessments, schooling is reduced to measures thought to determine the future success of the child. To be clear, "success" here does not refer to human flourishing or societal contribution, but to future monetary value (i.e., potential financial earnings) acquired through lucrative employment. Interestingly, this orientation also has the effect of recasting parents as shareholders vis-à-vis the future valuation of their children rather than stakeholders in their education. The school system's (and greater society's) hyper-focus on performance and a future-orientation of the value of some children and youth reflects the ways in which the investor (the state) seeks a return (future workers who contribute to the GDP and international competition) on its investment (public schooling). Here, the capital (students) is constructed in terms of individual value and success (determined through competition implicit within grades, standardized tests, and rankings), and as their future worth and worthiness. By recasting the purpose of education to be about a child's future capital worth, neoliberal policy reforms obscure and devalue the rational and relational essence of teaching.

Consistent with future valuing, there are those children, like Devan, who are persistently devalued in and by the educational system. For example, students who are already disadvantaged by social policies (outlined in this book's introduction and portrayed throughout the chapters), are greatly overrepresented in streams associated with learning and behaviour disabilities – what Martell (2020) terms "bottom streaming" – and underrepresented in socially valued programs. In Ontario, Parekh et al. (2011) found that streaming is "embedded within seemingly appropriate modifications to academic expectations such as within English as a Second Language programmes, Individual Educational Plans, and within programmes where expectations regarding both the quality of work and behaviour are greatly reduced" (p. 252). On the other hand, those streams which offer academic opportunities – French Immersion, Advanced Placement, and International Baccalaureate – were seen to enhance economic outcomes, thus creating "a small but dominant elite group" (p. 253). Parekh and her colleagues conclude that the system "apportions opportunities to students who already mirror the identity of those with economic power" (p. 273). Therefore, the effects of disenfranchisement experienced by children through their status of being a racialized minority, experiencing poverty, being in care, or having inequitable access to funding and supports is magnified in, through, and by the school system.

Under the miserable conditions (Brown, 2015) of diminished social and educational provision, increasing standardization, and greater demand for performativity of students and teachers – in the interest of accumulation, productivity, and competition (Gerwitz, 2002; Hursh, 2005) – teachers in our study described an "adiaphorized existence" (Bauman, 1999, p. 125), whereby teaching is rendered "neither good nor evil, measurable against technical (procedural) but not moral values" (p. 125). Due to a sense of an externally imposed direction that often carries little meaning for themselves, teachers' feelings of self-doubt, frustration, guilt, shame, and inadequacy represent a growing moral ambivalence about the purposes and consequences of their work. Teachers in this study could not let go of their attachments to certain "visceral beliefs about justice" (Flax, 1993, p. 7) and how their students should be treated. Yet holding on to those beliefs in morally neutralized bureaucracies – resource-led rather than needs-led – constituted a daily challenge. Were they really preserving the dignity and worthiness of each student? Or were they simply swimming against a tide "ordered by rationalization, bureaucracy and capitalism" (Brown, 2017, p. 63) that would eventually overwhelm them?

In these times, teachers are cast as witnesses to the workings and abuses of institutional power, the human cost of neglect, and the struggle to survive when social supports are no longer in existence for students and their families who have been already disenfranchised on the basis of (dis)ability, classism, and racism (Webb, Briscoe & Mussman, 2009). Masking their underlying political commitments (i.e., education as epiphenomenal to the economy), governments zoom in on so-called high standards and pre-set accountability goals that have already determined students' "realistic" identities and circumscribed their economic futures (De Lissovoy & McLaren, 2003). Teachers are rendered complicit in maintaining an "ethics of competition" (Hyneman Knight, 2017) in schools that create, legitimate, and sustain not only differentiated knowledge but stratified economic rewards and wealth. As a result, neoliberal economic theory relies on the continued discourse of merit, progress, and choice to justify its aims – positioning itself as a "'natural' occurrence of educational and economic behaviour" (Webb, Briscoe & Mussman, 2009, p. 5).

Within the current social and education policy environment, the teacher's commitment to care about the child's dignity, worth, and proximity, and to an openness for a future not yet known, is easily diluted. The ethical relation that anchors teaching is all but lost when a sense of future possibility for some children is foreclosed. This is the reason why teacher anxiety weaves itself through the pages of teachers' stories in this volume. Teachers experienced anxiety in the face of children in need because it was during those encounters when their own freedom to choose how to act became visceral. Teachers recounted experiences of worry and deep concern about how parents, colleagues, and school leaders might judge their actions. The sense of external demands and self-imposed expectations made many teachers feel alienated and isolated. Anxiety provokes consciousness of one's own professional identity and values and can inform teachers' choices, loyalties, and responsibilities. The possibility of doing nothing is always present, but the freedom to act can induce dread even as it evokes the realization of one's own commitments and freedoms. The moral person need *not* be destroyed. In the face of obligation, then, "the upside of anxiety" (Ruti, 2014, p. 141) is that it provokes and sustains the teacher's own singularity as an ethical subject – her irreplaceability and inimitability – summoning her beyond complacency towards response. In this sense, the anxiety of obligation need not be only a negative affect but can become a positive resource for teachers, a site of resolve and endurance.

Visceral moments of acute responsibility – encounters with obligation that threaten to overwhelm – provoked profound questions for teachers: Why isn't the system doing more for these students? Why is there so little support for families in need? Who is obligated to teachers at the end of the day? Why bother to teach if this is all there is? Is this teaching? For many teachers in our study, help never seemed to come; regardless, teachers continued to show up and did the best they could.

When teachers decided to resign, it was not that they had stopped caring about making a difference for children, nor did it necessarily mean that they were burnt out. Instead, it reflected the realization that they could only ever achieve an intimation of a truth that they longed for and pursued relentlessly – like trying to fill a leaky bucket. Some teachers recognized this challenge and concluded that fidelity to oneself is in the end impossible in today's schools. Meeting one's obligation is often simply unattainable. As such, the decision to leave was the only ethical decision remaining. Ethical because as an act of refusal – "an active 'not that'" – it is leaving that "actively interrupts the smooth operation of a normative order" (Carusi, 2017, p. 636). In leaving, teachers displace but refuse to replace norms so that the system is unable to "recuperate that ethical break" (p. 636).

It must be noted, however, that for those who decided to stay and also for those who eventually decided to leave the profession, teachers in this study found themselves having to constantly face their own vulnerability as persons and as educators. The question of leaving or staying is not just any question teachers are dealing with but a profound moral question about how one ought to live as an educator. At the core of leading a good and faithful life is the challenge of responding to the needs and suffering of others, a given in a human life. However, "[f]idelity to oneself is not for the fainthearted" (Lear, 2011, p. 5); this is especially so for teachers given the contemporary dominance of ideologies of the market and managerialism (Ball, 2003). The question of how one should live as a teacher within such miserable conditions involves an ongoing quest for meaning and significance.

Remaining in teaching for years on end while considering the possibility of leaving required a posture of endurance. Endurance calls for both tender-heartedness (as in the care or consideration of one to another living being) and a tough-mindedness about what happens in and to life (as in the destructiveness of all forms of life in war) (Heaney, 2013). Endurance embodies a hospitality that avoids overfamiliarity and the danger of becoming "immune to the intolerable" (Heaney, 2013). It demonstrates a resolve to be steadfast despite feelings of fragility and weariness; it reflects strength in the face of an acknowledgment of the challenges borne of living and teaching in an unsympathetic system. A teacher's resilience, however, should not be read as a solitary triumph. Like the sequoia redwood trees whose roots are relatively shallow but intertwined, teachers can stand tall if they have a community gathered around them. When teachers recalled the fellowship of practitioners with whom they had worked closely in the early years of their careers, they were not being nostalgic, they were pointing to the significance of colleagues as interlocutors in one's attempt to pursue meaningfulness, to achieve some clarity of purpose, and to compose an ethical life in teaching.

In light of the impact of current conditions on teachers, the profession cannot remain indifferent to pressing questions of purpose and meaning (vs. utility) in teaching. Unfortunately, policy has involved a standardization of the social and operational meanings of professional practice and teacher identity. This has meant, among other things, the emergence of a bureaucratic professionalism (Green, 1966), an attempt by some governments to regulate the very idea of what it means to be professional, sidestepping the ethico-political commitment that teaching entails. Obligation, as an ethical response to an urgent plea, is central to the concept of vocation; it is the ethos that characterizes the stories teachers tell in this volume.

Willing to face the "compromised conditions of possibility" (Berlant, 2011, p. 24) that beset many of their students, most teachers seemed to endure with integrity because of their capacity to trust the prospect of a different future for their students. This is not to say that their resolve never wavered, but it is to say they remained true to the possibility that school could be otherwise. They never fully succumbed to the language of performativity, and they held on to an idea of education as relation, albeit tenuously. We do not claim this for all teachers, of course; there are likely some teachers for whom the ethical has long been sidelined and for whom questioning the status quo is no longer a habit of mind.

While scholars may caution against a romanticization of teachers and teaching via a language of vocation, we argue that "discerning, articulating and culturing the vocation" of teaching "has rarely been so important … or neglected" (Brown, 2017, p. 59). It is important that we are reminded of the profession's "worldly purposes" – to educate by honouring the distinctiveness, cultivating the commitments, and preserving the dignity of each student – by teachers who refuse to become complicit "in a time and world increasingly voided of such purposes" (p. 60). Of course, refusal is not without its own abiding conflicts and contradictions, resulting from the desire to meet external expectations while achieving one's internal aspirations.

What can we learn from the teachers in this study about teaching as vocation, in all its complication? We focus on three aspects of vocation – commitment, resolve, and trust – that best characterize teachers' attempts to embrace the full humanity of their students and work against their institutional dehumanization.

A Teaching Vocation: Commitment, Resolve, and Trust

There is no doubt that vocation is a term with a complex history whose usage has changed, and changed again, over time. In keeping with Farrell & DeAne Lagerquist (2014), we believe that vocation is lived out within a specific time and place, in response to particular people, communities, and circumstances. As such, any contemporary articulation of teaching as a vocation has to be considered in relation to our capitalist economy, our culturally and religiously plural society, and our environmentally endangered world. This is no easy task given that vocation is most often associated with the Roman Catholic understanding of vocation as a calling to a religious way of life; a life that is Christ-centred, focused on discipleship, emulation, and charism or strength of character (O'Donoghue, 2014). In this view, a teacher with a calling or vocation is a role model whose effort to imitate the life of Christ is such that they inspire devotion in others. In the sixteenth century, Martin Luther arrived at a new understanding of the term (Schwehn and DeAne Lagerquist, 2014). Extending vocation to include any occupation as long as it was "enacted out of a Christian moral sensibility for the benefit of one's neighbor and the glorification of God" (p. 9), Martin Luther shifted the understanding of vocation from what one did to how and for whom one did it. Bricklaying could be a vocation, as could farming, nursing, mothering, or teaching.

Educational thinkers who have written about the call to teaching have focused on the relational quality of the profession. David Hansen (2021) elegantly describes the encounter between teacher, student, and the curriculum (the world): "Teaching means being with students and the particular subject at hand in a concern-full, engaged, and patient manner that is saturated with thinking, emotion, wondering, doubting, questioning, waiting, and more. A rich aesthetic, moral, and intellectual vocabulary enters the scene here, featuring terms like attunement to students' thought and feeling in relation to the subject; receptivity to what their words and actions imply; tact in listening and speaking with them; and responsiveness to their concerns, worries, and uncertainties" (p. 35). For Hansen, the teacher's very being as a teacher is a soulful *being with* the students, to "feel" the moment of encounter, and "to sense when to speak and when to listen" (p. 35). Attunement to students' thoughts and feelings requires passionate commitment.

Commitment

For the teachers in this study, the "subject at hand" presented in forms beyond that of the official curriculum and/or subject matter; it presented as life itself, the "concerns, worries and uncertainties" (Hansen, 2021, p. 35) that children and youth bring with them to school as well as those they encounter while there. What was foremost for teachers was commitment to individual students; a "concern with or care for [each child's] coming into being … not exhausted in its objectivity but … disclosed in relationships" (Løvlie, 2002, p. 484). When Stacey told us that she had "decided to make [her] mission to engage, nurture and love" the student Chris, she was expressing a commitment to be *for* him. Or, when Lena refused to apply the specialist's recommendations, she did so in order to protect and defend seven-year-old James; displaying her single-minded dedication to his well-being in the present as well as in the future.

The encounter between teacher and student is primarily an encounter between persons – arguably the essence of human living that is under threat in bureaucracies. "[T]he form that this encounter takes is the meaning of life" itself (Huebner, 1999, p. 110). "The encounter is not *used* to produce change, to enhance prestige, to identify new knowledge, or to be symbolic of something else. The encounter *is*. In it is the essence of life. In it life is revealed and lived. The student is not viewed as an object, an *it*; but as a fellow human being, another subject, a *thou*, who is to be lived with in the fullness of the present moment or the eternal present" (p. 110; italics in the original). As such, students' encounters with each other, the world around them, and the teacher constitute the fullness of the educational activity: the encounter is all there is. "The educational activity is life – and life's meanings are witnessed and lived in the classroom" (Huebner, 1999, p. 110). The value of the educational act per se, not its significance for other ends (e.g., human capital), or the realization of other values, is key. We are not suggesting that a deep and long-lasting personal relationship needs to form between teachers and students. What obligation asks of a teacher is to "be totally and non-selectively present to the student – to each student – as he [*sic*] addresses me. The time interval may be brief but the encounter total" (Noddings, 1984, p. 180).

During encounters such as those between Patricia and Devan, Stacey and Chris, or Lena and James, which demand a great deal of emotional labour from both adult and child, there is little time to wonder about the failure of social policy, the sheer difficulty of growing up in institutions, the challenges of parenting in these times, or of simply staying alive. Rather, teachers are compelled to "lend a hand when the damage threatens to run beyond control, to help restore the possibility of joy, the rhythm of ordinary things" for vulnerable students (Caputo, 1993, p. 243). Sociologist Max Weber (2004) understood that such vocations require "the freely chosen commitment of individuals," to responsible work in the service of something greater than ourselves (Owen & Strong, 2004, p. xiii). An "ardent passion" or commitment was necessary in an "august human endeavour" that is often incredibly difficult but "potentially world-changing" (Weber, 2004, p. 8). In fact, he believed that without passionate commitment one simply could not possess a vocation. Those, like Lena or Stacey, with a vocation may appear strangely intoxicated – *overly* conscientious, committed or caring – and outsiders may "greet [them] with a pitying smile" (p. 8), but for Weber passion is directly proportional to the value one has for the activity in question.

Moreover, it is passion that sustains one's pursuit of clarity as to what is of value and motivates one to seek out the meaning of one's actions. What is involved is an *"orientation to truth"* (Owen & Strong, 2004, p. xxxii) in one's professional life whereby one tries to understand one's circumstances and commitments and to achieve an internal clarity of purpose in relation to external conditions.

Resolve

Weber recognized the importance of acknowledging historically specific conditions that shape vocations. There is, what Brown (2017) terms, "a sober idealism and *amor fati*" in Weber's thinking about vocations, "both a steely-eyed confrontation with existing conditions and a forceful rejection of them as determinant" (p. 58). Part of the intellectual integrity of one who takes up a vocation is one's undaunted acknowledgment of the realities of the particular historical era and the subsequent obligations such realities impose (Owen & Strong, 2004). In fact, Weber (2004) goes so far as to assert that one's life has ethical meaning insofar as one acknowledges the circumstances and related commitments.

Facing the cold hard facts of any situation not only deprives us of illusions from which we might draw comfort, it paradoxically provides the necessary ground and potential of our agency. Weber (2004) cautioned, however, that historical conditions can intensify a dangerous desire for certainty; the desire to fix what are unfixable human affairs will inevitably lead to dismay and bitter indignation. This does not mean that one can do nothing. In fact, acknowledgment of one's reality imbues one with an even deeper sense of responsibility that "shapes commitment, animates conduct, and establishes restraint" when necessary (Brown, 2015, p. 65). Justin confronts the remnants of cultural genocide in his Northern location: a white teaching staff largely disengaged from the Indigenous community it served; insufficient public funding for much needed Arts programming; and no extra-curricular activities for youth. As a teacher in only the second year of his career, Justin reveals the double responsibility that characterizes vocational activity: to both enact and cultivate mature adulthood in oneself with the support of one's students and their families. As Weber (2004) states: "I find it immeasurably moving when a mature [*reif*] human being – whether young or old in actual years is immaterial – who feels the responsibility he [*sic*] bears for the consequences of his own actions with his [*sic*] entire soul and who acts in harmony with an ethics of responsibility reaches the point where he [*sic*] says, 'Here I stand, I can do no other.' That is authentically human and cannot fail to move us [*ergreift*]" (p. 92). The resolve to stand in solidarity with one's students and their families in the face of challenging circumstances that require more of a teacher than is usual – participating in extensive fundraising for new school programs or in protests against school closure – is as impressive as it is paradoxical.

As citizens of the modern state, teachers and students exist in the shadow of coercive power, but teachers are directly implicated in the violence of the state (Casson, 2014). The decisions teachers make and the policies they enact are inextricably linked to the exercise of power (Casson, 2014). When person-to-person encounters occur, those involved may find themselves operating outside of prescribed institutional roles; ironically, the teacher may become unrecognizable as such. There are times when resolve requires that teachers "suspend the relatively organized structure of our identity by letting ourselves fall into a less organized state of being" (Ruti, 2014, p. 123). These are times when they feel so powerfully called to respond that they may feel as if they have no choice but to answer. There is no room for deliberation. These moments invoke a desire that undoes a conscious desire to flee, to remove oneself from the situation (Caputo, 1993). Just about to leave school for the day, a teacher receives a phone call from the police telling him about the student's imminent release from hospital and the parents' refusal to have their son back in their home after his recent suicide attempt. The moment of resolve is as "terrifying as it is exhilarating" (Ruti, 2014,

p. 124) as the teacher, Doug, immediately drives to the hospital to pick up Stephen, his grade twelve student.

Ted Tetsuo Aoki's (2004) moving depiction of one teacher's resolve during a period of Japanese internment in Canada comes to mind here. Mr. McNab stood watching his Japanese students depart the two-roomed schoolhouse on Vancouver Island knowing that he might never see them again. It was 1942 and the children, with their families, would soon make another journey to the Japanese Internment Camp somewhere in the interior of British Columbia. Aoki's characterization of the teacher's "pedagogical watchfulness" (p. 195) combines passionate concern alongside a sober resolve: "It was a watching that was watchfulness – a watchfulness filled with a teacher's hope that wherever his students may be; wherever they may wander on this earth away from his presence, they are well and no harm will visit them" (p. 195). Aoki's story depicts what Huebner (1999) articulates: that to embrace teaching as vocation is "to find one's life and work participating in the formation of another's story, and vice versa" (p. 382). In this sense, the teacher is "relationally captive" (van Manen, 2012, p. 12) – for in the immediacy of pedagogical moments, teachers surrender to the Other in such a way that "quite literally our mind is not our own" (p. 12). Resolve reflects the rational *and* the relational in teaching.

Trust

Obligation, as a form of ethical responsibility, is primordial because it is situated outside the limits of human reason (Biesta, 2006). Obligation involves being responsible "for what is to come, without knowledge of what is to come" (p. 148). Teachers in this study cling, as it were, to a "perhaps" – a desire, a belief, a wish that sometime, in the future, things might be otherwise for their students. They demonstrate faith in the unexpected (Phelan & Janzen, 2021). They are open to the unforeseen.

In a densely populated urban neighbourhood, Ian confronts the harsh realities facing non-English-speaking, immigrant students trying to succeed in an under-resourced public school. Feeling compelled to stay but understanding of colleagues who chose to leave to teach elsewhere, Ian's story testifies to the demands of teaching as a vocation – "an unconditional faithfulness" (Ruti, 2014, p. 128). It asks teachers, as ethical subjects, to hold their ground and not to betray it via laziness, indifference, or fear when others tell them that its "calling requires too much devotion or dedication or is itself an illusion that may take us in harmful directions" (p. 128). To answer a calling, to succumb to obligation, is not the same as self-sacrifice, however. We are not suggesting that teachers relinquish professional autonomy and embrace dangerous saviour fantasies. Neither do we wish to patronize teachers by asserting their courage in the face of "exhaustingly difficult" work where "rewards … remain sometimes intangible, often rare, and always uncertain" (Block, 2014, p. 54). Ours is not an ideology of self-abnegation that demands that teaching is all about the students, obscuring teachers' own interests and motivations even from themselves (Grumet, 2014). Our interest here is in openness.

Contrary to discourses of neoliberalism, the teacher's faith in a different yet unknown future for students is given not as an investment expecting a return, but rather as a "gift" (Caputo, 2012). As Caputo explains, the "innumerable, invisible, ghostly gifts the teachers make are all gratuitous, extra, in excess of the economy, yet they are all absolutely necessary. The gift must be given, yet it is not a gift if it is compelled, coerced, demanded" (p. 25) – just like Mr. McNab's watchfulness on that fateful day or Tara's attempts to minimize student shame by distracting them with little care packages – loot bags – on report card day. Obligation summons faithfulness to the unexpected (Caputo, 2012) when disappointment in a system and a sense of inadequacy in one's self might seem more reasonable.

Believing in what might be possible in the midst of the impossible is an act of faith (Phelan & Janzen, 2021). Faith in the unexpected is challenging and depends on the often imperceptible but powerful presence of others – the ones who come bearing the gift of hospitality; the ones we didn't expect. Recall the support Justin received from members of the Indigenous community: what he called the community's "system of care."

Teaching as a vocation is about being willing to welcome "newness and surprise, pain and happiness," for these, Huebner (1999) writes, "are dimensions of the world that make us rethink, almost daily, who and what we are" (p. 380). Teaching is an ongoing and ever unfinished project of the self who answers a call. A teaching vocation summons a person to create and recreate personal meaning that lends weight and worthiness to their existence. It emphasizes the importance of one's own assessment of what matters (judgment) on the basis of loyalty to an always inaccessible "good." It is about "living intentionally and openly, not routinely" (p. 380).

The idea of vocation, therefore, is both active and passive: the teacher must freely give of herself to that which calls but by responding to that call she is shaped by and appears as. Stacey's nightmare testifies to the degree to which obligation inserts itself in teachers' interior lives. As both defining and expressive of the teacher, the idea of vocation provokes a complicated ethics of singularity. Singularity is "less a nameable quality than an inscrutable intensity of being" (Ruti, 2012, p. 9). It acknowledges the unending and precarious task of composing and recomposing a self that feels authentic or meaningful despite the pull of circumstance. In this regard, we bring this chapter to a close with one more teacher's story.

Experiencing and Resisting Bureaucratization: A Closing Tale

Jennifer was an early years educator with over thirty years of teaching experience. She described herself as having "a deep-rooted feeling or belief" in teaching in the best interests of children: "I was there to learn about the children and my teaching would be based on what I knew about these kids." Recalling the "clique of passionate teachers" with whom she practised during the early years of her career, and with whom she had a history of pedagogical innovation, dialogue, and mentoring, she expressed anxiety over district policies that had taken hold more recently. She cited mandatory standardized (developmental) testing and imposed behaviour control programs as reflecting a lack of responsiveness to young children and those most in need. These policies and programs not only re-described what it meant to be an early years educator, they mandated that teachers like Jennifer teach against their own value set.

Angered by the imposition of standardized testing, Jennifer assumed an advocacy role; analysing issues and problems in district policy and designing blueprints for practice. For example, she repeatedly sent letters to the district superintendent coupled with samples of student work to illustrate both the negative impact of the new assessment protocols and to offer alternatives; her intent was to provoke dialogue and achieve, at the very least, a suspension or modification of policy. Her advocacy was both educational and ethical, protecting children from those forces that did not seem to operate in their best interests and, in her own words, "guard[ing] them from outside influences like whole-school decisions," which she deemed harmful. Her efforts were repeatedly met with the indifference of a faceless bureaucracy. No offer for dialogue was ever made. No response ever issued from the superintendent's office to Jennifer's letters.

Over time, Jennifer's dream that things could be otherwise – "to make justice imaginable again" (Camus, 1948, p. 135) – became wearied by "the callousness of reality" (Heaney, 2013). It was difficult to sustain a sense of possibility under such circumstances; she felt isolated, no longer having a professional circle to support her, and muted in a system where policy norms took precedence over teachers' expressed concerns about the perceived impacts of policy on children. By the time we talked with Jennifer, she seemed to have lost a sense of what it meant to be a teacher.

Jennifer had tried to navigate a course between being a perpetual disrupter of policy norms and becoming cynically detached from her commitment to children. However, in the end, she could not remain in a school district where the moral face of teaching had been stripped away. Jennifer's eventual decision to leave teaching was visceral. In our interview with her, she remembered the moment when she finally decided she could teach no longer. She was cleaning up after Michel, a grade two child in her class, who was still "pooping in his pants" [and] was "very active and baby-like … tactile," and had defaecated during a classroom activity. Faced with a child with such desperate needs and with no assistance or means to support him, Jennifer found herself in moral distress; the constraints on her intractable. She decided to leave teaching for good.

Ironically, it is in a moment of ethical obligation to a child, that Jennifer turned away from teaching after over three decades. It was a moment of bodily interference, of confusion about what constitutes teaching, and the implied expectation that she should not only implement what she considered mis-educative policies but also to continue to work ethically with children for whom there were no adequate supports. It is the unfeeling indifference of systems to the plight of children and teachers that is striking here. Such moments remind teachers that they have strayed (or have been led) far from the aspirations they once held.

In teaching, obligation underscores the singular and concrete quality of teachers' ethical responses. Yet, in the preceding chapters of this book, we have witnessed the increasing reliance on general or abstract policies, professional codes of conduct, and teaching standards to determine teachers' judgments and actions. Teachers described the challenge of being ethically responsive in schools and school districts where daily activity was conducted in bureaucratic terms, that is, according to impersonal rules and "without regard for persons" (Weber, 1978, p. 954). The indifference towards persons means the erasure of all personal, irrational, and emotional elements of living; schools and classrooms become "de-enchanted" (Kemple, 2014, p. 230). As a form of human organization, bureaucracies operate as if action and its consequences can be premeditated and established in advance of any human encounter. In the bureaucratic denial of unpredictability, it is believed that responsibility can be defined and codified prior to contact between persons also; as such, bureaucratic institutions demand compliance rather than invite situated moral judgment. Caputo (1993) argues against the equation of obedience to norms with responsibility, writing: "obedience is not necessarily responsible; it depends on what you obey. Sometimes responding to the call of the other requires the most scaring, disturbing disobedience to the law. Sometimes it is anarchy that is the most responsible of all" (p. 120). Anarchy underlies many of the stories recounted in this volume: teachers who refuse to collaborate with specialists or those who refuse to adhere to the professional codes of conduct or those, like Jennifer, who are unwilling to comply with district policies in an attempt to combat the dehumanization and alienation of their students and themselves.

Obligation is a call of character; it has "a vocational force," provoking teachers, evoking their response, and potentially transforming them (Caputo, 2012, p. 31). Many teachers would rather attempt to push against bio-power, that power that attempts to take hold of life, sustaining and regulating it, and refuse to be an instrument of others' intentions. Visceral responses on the part of teachers suggest that teachers are never simple docile instruments of normative orders. Both perpetrators of mundane violence (e.g., shaming) and subjects of excessive acts of care, teachers live agonistically often with their own colleagues, in order to answer the call of obligation in teaching. Our conversations with them suggest that teachers feel primarily obliged to students, secondarily to the profession, and not at all to the systems (i.e., represented by superintendents or school boards) in which they teach. Teachers expressed some ambivalence about their teaching colleagues who often represented the imperative to comply with norms and standards. All in all, however, and this is where hope resides, perhaps: rules and regulations did not override teachers' ethical response (Todd, 2003). Most teachers remained persuaded that there is a reason to teach and it is not just reason itself (Farrell & De Ane Lagerquist, 2014).

Conclusion

To revitalize a conversation about teaching as a vocation constitutes an attempt, at the very least, to counter overly simplistic discourses of teacher burnout and, at the very best, to re-establish that ethical obligation haunts teaching. As such, obligation attacks the teacher's sense of balance (Cavarero, 2016), but it also loosens the restrictive grip of normative demands of institutions and policies characterized by a distaste of human dependency and vulnerability.

Thinking about teaching in terms of commitment, resolve, and trust raises many questions during these post-pandemic times. A position paper titled *Teaching and Teacher Education for a Post-Pandemic Canada,* issued by the Association of Canadian Deans of Education (ACDE) (2020), identifies women as "leading the educational response" (ACDE, 2020, p. 6). Not an unreasonable statement, as the document points out, given that women constitute 84 per cent of the education profession. The figure of the female teacher is positioned at the nexus of a risk/safety discourse, being simultaneously the figure upon whom "moving forward" relies *and* the one who most threatens post-pandemic prosperity (Phelan & Morris, 2021). Women are a threat because they "carry much of the home responsibilities" and are at greater risk of infection and job loss (ACDE, 2020, p. 6). Self-sacrifice and a willingness to overwork are implicitly lauded as "capabilities" – what teachers can and will have to do – that require resilience in order to maintain "student learning in a time of pandemic crisis and recovery" (p. 9). The idea of resilience suggests holding the course in the face of difficulty and returning to original form afterwards (Phelan & Morris, 2021). Such entrapment of the teacher as an instrument of "positive change" (ACDE, 2020, p. 10), defined in terms of "Canada's post-pandemic economic performance through human capital, innovation, and knowledge transfer" (p. 11), is not what we have in mind when we speak of teachers' commitment, resolve, and trust in the future.

Rather, we acknowledge the existence of teachers who struggle daily with the question of what it means to live one's life in teaching with fidelity. How to sustain such a vocational life is less clear. No one can tell Jennifer or Patricia what to do, how to respond to the children in their care, or provide arguments on how to live their lives in teaching. This is something they and we must seek for ourselves, inspired by a passionate commitment, a sober resolve, and a willingness to take a leap of faith when obligation summons.

However, we also acknowledge the collective responsibility of organizations such as the Association of the Canadian Deans of Education, the Canadian Federation of Teachers, as well as other professional and academic bodies to bear witness to the miserable conditions in which teachers teach and to raise public awareness of the same. Neoliberal rationality is in the process of remaking our children, their teachers, and ourselves in the image of *homo oeconomicus*. It is transposing constitutive elements of Canadian democracy – education, law, governance – into an economic register. Wendy Brown's (2015) warning that the *demos* – the common people or the public – is being overtaken by a new common sense is palpable in teachers' stories. It is this neoliberal reason that generates the very miserable conditions that provoke consideration of the vocational qualities of teaching. However, vocational qualities such as commitment, resolve, and trust, though significant for the connectivity they can generate among teachers, students, and communities, will continue to be undermined by neoliberal educational and social policy. The erosion of democracy is well underway. Where will this story end? What will education look like in the future? What will it mean for teachers? Who will act? As a starting point, governments, professional and academic organizations, school districts, communities, and families need to engage in substantive conversations about what matters educationally; and to consider collectively: What is education for? What is it we want for our children – and our world? How will we know that what we want is desirable?

References

Aoki, T. (2004). Layered voices of teaching: The uncannily correct and the elusively true. In W.F. Pinar & R. Irwin (Eds.), *Curriculum in a new key: The collected works of Ted T. Aoki* (pp. 189–97). Taylor & Francis. (Original work published 1992)

Association of Canadian Deans of Education (2020). *Teaching and teacher education for a post-pandemic Canada*. ACDE Publication.

Ball, S.J. (2003). The teacher's soul and the terrors of performativity. *Journal of Education Policy, 18*(2), 215–28. https://doi.org/10.1080/0268093022000043065

Bauman, S. (1999). *Liquid modernity*. Polity Press.

Berlant, L. (2011). *Cruel optimism*. Duke University Press.

Biesta, G. (2006). *Beyond learning: Democratic education for a human future*. Paradigm.

Block, A. (2014). *The classroom: Encounter and engagement*. Palgrave Macmillan.

Borman, G.D., & Kimball, S. (2005). Teacher quality and educational equality: Do teachers with higher standards-based evaluation ratings close student achievement gaps? *Elementary School Journal, 106*(1), 3–20. https://doi.org/10.1086/496904

British Columbia Teachers Federation (2021). The FSA: A measure of inequity. https://www.bctf.ca/whats-happening/news-details/2021/11/04/the-fsa-a-measure-of-inequity

Brown, W. (2015). *Undoing the demos: Neoliberalism's stealth revolution*. Zone Books.

– (2017). The vocation of the public university. In A.B. Jørgensen, J.J. Justesen, N. Bech, N. Nykrog, & R.B. Clemmensen (Eds.), *What is education? An anthology on education* (pp. 55–89). Problema.

Camus, A. (1948). *The plague*. Modern Library Edition.

Caputo, J. (1993). *Against ethics: Contributions to a poetics with constant reference to deconstruction*. Indiana University Press.

– (2012). Teaching the event: Deconstruction, hauntology, and the scene of pedagogy. In C. W. Ruitenberg (Ed.), *Philosophy of education yearbook* (pp. 23–34). Philosophy of Education Society.

Carusi, F.T. (2017). Why bother teaching? Despairing the ethical through teaching that does not follow. *Studies in Philosophy of Education, 36*, 633–45. https://doi.org/10.1007/s11217-017-9569-0

Casson, D. (2014). On teaching politics as vocation. In K. Schwehn & L.D. Lagerquist (Eds.), *Claiming our callings: Toward a new understand of vocation in the liberal arts*. Oxford Scholarship OnLine. https://doi.org/10.1093/acprof:oso/9780199341047.001.0001

Cavarero, A. (2016). *Inclinations: A critique of rectitude*. SpringerLink.

Connell, R. (2009). Good teachers on dangerous ground: Toward a new view of teacher quality and professionalism. *Critical Studies in Education, 50*(3), 213–29. https://doi.org/10.1080/17508480902998421

Crocco, M.S., & Costigan, A.T. (2007). The narrowing of curriculum and pedagogy in the age of accountability urban educators speak out. *Urban Education*, 42(6), 512–35. https://doi.org/10.1177/0042085907304964

Day, C., & Gu, Q. (2010). *The new lives of teachers*. Routledge.

De Lissovoy, N., & McLaren, P. (2003). Educational 'accountability' and the violence of capital: A Marxian reading. *Journal of Education Policy, 18*(2), 131–43. https://doi.org/10.1080/0268093022000043092

Farrell J., & Lagerquist, L.D. (2014). Afterword. In K. Schwehn & L.D. Lagerquist (Eds.), *Claiming our callings: Toward a new understand of vocation in the liberal arts*. Oxford Scholarship OnLine. https://doi.org/10.1093/acprof:oso/9780199341047.001.0001

Ferguson, R.F. (1998). Can schools narrow the Black-White test score gap? In C. Jencks & M. Phillips (Eds.), *The Black-White test score gap* (pp. 318–74). Brookings Institution.

Flax, J. (1993). *Disputed subjects: Essays on psychoanalysis, politics and philosophy*. Routledge.

Fraser, N. (July/August 2016). Contradictions of capital and care. *New Left Review, 100*, 99–117.

Gerwitz, S. (2002). *The managerial school: Post-welfarism and social justice in education*. Routledge.

Green, A.D. (1966). The professional social worker in the bureaucracy. *Social Service Review, 40*(1): 71–83. https://doi.org/10.1086/641857

Greene, M. (1988). What are the Language Arts for? *Language Arts, 65*(5), 474–81.

Grumet, M.R. (2014). The question of teacher education. *Learning Landscapes, 8*(1), 21–6. https://doi.org/10.36510/learnland.v8i1.670

Hansen, D.T. (2021). *Reimagining the call to teach: A witness to teachers and teaching*. Teachers College Press.

Heaney, S. (30 August 2013). *From the stacks: Crediting poetry*. The 1995 Nobel Lecture. *The New Republic*. https://newrepublic.com/article/114540/seamus-heaneys-crediting-poetry-nobel-lecture
Huebner, D. (1999). Curricular language and classroom meanings (1966). In V. Hillis & W.F. Pinar (Eds.), *The lure of the transcendent: Collected essays by Dwayne Huebner* (pp. 101–17). Routledge.
– (1999). Teaching as a vocation (1987). In V. Hillis & W.F. Pinar (Eds), *The lure of the transcendent: Collected essays by Dwayne Huebner* (pp. 379–87). Routledge.
Hursh, D. (2005). Neo-liberalism, markets and accountability: Transforming education and undermining democracy in the United States and England. *Policy Futures in Education, 3*(1), 3–15. https://doi.org/10.2304/pfie.2005.3.1.6
Kain, J.F., & Singleton, K. (May–June 1996). Equality of educational opportunity revisited. *New England Economic Review*, 87–111.
Kemple, T. (2014). *Intellectual work and the spirit of capitalism: Weber's calling*. Palgrave Macmillan.
Kersaint, G., Lewis, J., Potter, R., & Meisels, G. (2007). Why teachers leave: Factors that influence retention and resignation. *Teaching and Teacher Education, 23*(6), 775–94. https://doi.org/10.1016/j.tate.2005.12.004
Klees, S.J. (2020). Beyond neoliberalism: Reflections on capitalism and education. *Policy Futures in Education, 18*(1), 9–29. https://doi.org/10.1177/1478210317715814
Lear, J. (2011) *A case for irony*. Harvard University Press.
Loeb, S., Darling-Hammond, L., & Luczak, J. (2005). How teaching conditions predict teacher turnover in California schools. *Peabody Journal of Education, 80*(3), 44–70. https://doi.org/10.1207/s15327930pje8003_4
Løvlie, L. (2002) The promise of Bildung. *Journal of Philosophy of Education, 36*(3), 467–86. https://doi.org/10.1111/1467-9752.00288
Martell, G. (2020). There is no de-streaming without democracy and meaning. *School Magazine: Education Action Toronto*. https://educationactiontoronto.com/articles/there-is-no-de-streaming-without-democracy-and-meaning / January 9.
Noddings, N. (1984). *Caring: A relational approach to ethics and moral education*. University of California Press.
O'Donoghue, T. (2014). The contemporary Catholic teacher: A reappraisal of the concept of teaching as a vocation in the Catholic Christian context. *International Studies in Catholic Education, 6*(2), 209–11. https://doi.org/10.1080/19422539.2014.929786
Owen, D., & Strong, T.B. (2004). Introduction: Max Weber's calling to knowledge and action. In D. Owen & T.B. Strong (Eds.), *The vocation lectures* (R. Livingstone, Trans.). (pp. ix–lxii). Hackett.

Parekh, G, Killoran, I., & Crawford, C. (2011). The Toronto connection: Poverty, perceived ability, and access to education equity. *Canadian Journal of Education, 34*(3), 249–79.

Parker, L. (2017). Creating a crisis: Selling neoliberal policy through the rebranding of education. *Canadian Journal of Educational Administration and Policy, 183*, 44–60.

Phelan, A.M., & Janzen, M.D. (2021). Faith in the unexpected: The event of obligation in teaching. *Learning Landscapes, 14*(1), 305–15. https://doi.org/10.36510/learnland.v14i1.1037

Phelan, A.M., & Morris, J. (2021). Teaching and teacher education for a post-pandemic Canada: Context, crisis, critique, complication. In Diane Mayer (Ed.), *Teacher education policy and research: Global perspectives* (pp. 43–56). Springer.

Ruti, M. (2012). *The singularity of being: Lacan and the immortal within*. Fordham University Press.

– (2014). *The call of character: Living a life worth living*. Columbia University Press.

Schwehn, K., & DeAne Lagerquist, L. (Eds.). (2014). *Claiming our callings: Toward a new understand of vocation in the liberal arts*. Oxford Scholarship OnLine. https://doi.org/10.1093/acprof:oso/9780199341047.001.0001

Steeves, L., Carr-Stewart, S., Kirk, J., & Prytula, M. (2013). *Teacher recruitment and retention in rural, northern, and Aboriginal communities in Western Canada*. Paper presented at the Canadian Society for the Study of Education Annual Conference.

Todd, S. (2003). *Learning from the other: Levinas, psychoanalysis, and ethical possibilities in education*. The State University of New York Press.

United Nations (2015). Sustainable development goals. https://www.un.org/sustainabledevelopment/blog/2015/06/give-young-people-decent-jobs-and-they-will-create-a-better-future-un-chief/

van Manen, M. (2012). The call of pedagogy as the call of contact. *Phenomenology & Practice, 6*(2), 8–34. https://doi.org/10.29173/pandpr19859

Webb, P.T., Briscoe, F.M., & Mussman, M.P. (2009). Preparing teachers for the neoliberal panopticon. *Educational Foundations*, Summer/Fall, pp. 1–16.

Weber, M. (1978). *Economy and society*. University of California Press.

– (2004). *Politics as vocation*. In D. Owen & T.B. Strong (Eds.), *The vocation lectures* (R. Livingstone, Trans.) (pp. 32–94). Hackett.

Index

accountability, 14, 28, 31, 105, 107
affect, 19, 61–8; and conflict, 91–2; negative affect, 107
Ahmed, Sara, 62–4
alterity, 38–41, 53
anarchy, 118
anxiety, 10, 20, 46–7, 92–3, 98–9, 107, 116
Aoki, Ted Tetsuo, 114
assessment, 27, 30–2, 59, 105, 116
attrition, 4–5, 45, 104

bad feelings, 74, 95–7, 99
Ball, Stephen, 17, 31, 94, 108
Berlant, Lauren, 55, 62–3, 65, 99, 109
Biesta, Gert, 59, 114
Britzman, Deborah, 20, 47, 55, 91–3, 99–100
Brown, Wendy, 7, 8, 12, 20, 104, 106–7, 109, 112, 119
bureaucracy, 20, 107, 116; bureaucratization, 116
burnout, 5, 75–6, 118
Butler, Judith, 17, 28–30, 35–7, 41–2, 55, 93

Caputo, John, 9–11, 19, 41. *See also* obligation
care, 20, 61, 77–80, 82–5; continuity of, 49; duty of, 4; eccentricities of, 77–9; economy of, 73–7; lack of, 49; natural, 74; and power, 85–8
children in care, 12–14, 38, 45
colonialism, 15
commitment, 20, 31, 40–3, 46–7, 50, 54, 110–13, 118–19; emotional, 104; political, 107, 109; unconditional, 83
community, 79–83, 109, 115
competition, 12, 59; academic, 65–6; international, 105; logic of, 62
complaint, 98
courage, 53–5, 68, 115
curriculum, 27–30, 34, 93, 110–11

death, 19, 73, 76, 79, 83
demoralization, 47, 49, 51
deprivation, 19, 36
Derrida, Jacques, 47–8
deviance, 42
différend, 82
disengagement (from the profession), 4–5, 45, 52, 55
disobedience, 46, 50–2, 118
distrust, 32, 47, 50–1
diversity, 45, 69, 104
doubt 40, 77, 100; self-doubt, 94–5, 106
dream, 91–2, 116; bad dreams, 19, 95, 98–9

education funding, 12, 14–16, 86, 106, 113
emotionality, 17, 28, 100
empathy, 38
encounters, 17, 37, 43, 107–17
English language learners, 81, 86, 106
ethics, 9–11, 53, 60; of responsibility, 113; of shame, 66–8; of singularity, 116
evaluation, 19, 32, 59–60, 66–9
expert, 28–34

failure, 5, 51, 66, 92–4; fear of, 105
fatalism, 60, 63, 69
fidelity, 55, 108, 119
financialization, 104
frames, 18, 28, 35–9, 42–3
Freud, Sigmund, 19, 91
future-orientation, 105

guilt, 34, 40, 61, 65, 106

Hansen, David, 6–8, 110–11
hope, 53, 101, 119
Huebner, Dwayne, 111, 114–15
humiliation, 59, 62

imagination, 46, 52, 54
immigrant students, 13, 81, 114
inequity, 16, 20, 36
international homestay students, 19, 73, 77, 86
intimacy, 76, 83–5

judgement, 9–10, 18, 28, 29, 30–3

Lingis, Alfonso, 73, 76–9, 83–5

madness, 19, 73, 87
managerialism, 17, 32, 108
marketization, 93
mastery, 28–9, 35, 42
monetization, 104
moral ambivalence, 106
moralism, 75–6

narrative, 5–6, 27, 32, 42, 69; counter, 68
neoliberalism, 4, 11–12, 15, 20, 85, 104, 115
Noddings, Nel, 73–4, 83
novelty, 69–70

obligation, 9–11, 17–20; as an appeal to pity, 74–7; as ethical responsibility, 114–18; as event, 80; as a form of attending, 69; as incessant demand, 45–6, 50, 52; and its effects, 91–2; Latin meaning of, 29; as a leap of faith, 76–80, 85, 119–20; meeting, 108; as minimizing harm, 18–19, 68–9; and phronesis, 74–5; and power, 85–7; and precarity, 28; teacher's, 47, 54–5, 82, 111; and undecidability, 82. *See also* Caputo, John.
Oliver, Kelly, 8, 50, 53–5, 94
openness, 28, 37–9, 41–2

parents, 31, 60, 63–9, 77, 82, 98–100; and neoliberalism, 105–6
performativity, 31–2, 93–4, 106, 109
Phillips, Adam, 20, 94, 96–9, 101
Pinar, William, 11, 20
policy, 4, 9, 14, 93; fiscal conservative, 15–16; neoliberal, 106–9, 116–17, 120; and policymakers, 81, 104
politics, 8, 60; of shame, 63–6, 69
poverty, 16, 19, 36, 106; and children, 12–13, 45–6, 104
powerlessness, 52, 69, 78, 82
practical wisdom (*phronesis*), *74*
Probyn, Elspeth, 61–2, 70
psychoanalysis, 36
punishment, 98–9

recognition, 37–8, 69; children's, 35–6; recognizability, 17, 28; as a teacher, 31–2. *See also* frames
relationships, 18; with children, 27–8, 32–4; and difference, 38, 41
report cards, 18, 59, 67–70
resistance, 38, 43, 55
resolve, 20, 107–10, 112–14, 118–19
responsibility, 3–4, 9–10; burden of, 94; for children, 46, 49, 53; collective, 119; for education, 27; for the Other, 54; as primordial, 114; and responsibilization, 93; society's, 17; and teachers, 96, 108, 113
responsiveness, 9, 55, 110; lack of, 116; teachers', 28, 49; visceral, 10
risk, 10; of breaking promises, 48–9; as enabling, 54; of ethical relation, 40–2; risk/safety discourse, 119
Ruti, Mari, 20, 80, 83–4, 94–5, 98, 101

school closure, 76, 81–2, 113
scrutiny, 31; self-scrutiny, 98
solidarity, 113
standardization, 28, 105–6; of meaning, 109
standardized tests, 62; testing, 105
subjection, 30
subjectivity, 8, 33, 97; teacher, 29, 32
suicide, 19, 76, 95, 113
surveillance (teacher), 31–2, 42, 51–2, 93; and children, 35, 67

Todd, Sharon, 30, 32–4, 37–42, 49, 53, 55, 92, 118
Tomkins, Silvan, 61
trust, 114–16
Tuck, Eve, 15

uncertainty, 10, 18, 20, 28, 29, 30; and ethics, 50; perpetual, 54–5; tolerance for, 43
undecidability, 29–30, 82
unrecognizability, 53

van Manen, Max, 19, 73, 114
violence, 28, 34, 118
Visser, Margaret, 60–1
vulnerability, 37, 40, 69, 78, 118; student's, 7, 67, 70; teacher's, 42, 48, 54

Weber, Max, 112–13, 117
Winnicott, Donald, 100
witnessing, 7–9, 53, 81
women, 14–15, 119; women's work, 99

Printed and bound by CPI Group (UK) Ltd, Croydon, CR0 4YY
29/09/2024
14565434-0001